GOOD HOUSEKEEPING

Preparing for Christmas

GOOD HOUSEKEEPING

Preparing for Christmas

Recipes and countdowns, menus
and party ideas, gifts and decorations –
the complete practical guide

HILARY ROBINSON

LIMITED EDITIONS

This edition published in 1994 by Limited Editions
by arrangement with Ebury Press
an imprint of Random House UK Ltd
Random House
20 Vauxhall Bridge Road
London SW1V 2SA

0 09 181867 2

Art Editor: Nick Dixon

Designer: Christine Wood
Editor: Barbara Croxford
Illustrations: Anthony Sidwell

Typeset by SX Composing Ltd
Printed and bound in Italy by New Interlitho Italia, S.p.a., Milan

Contents

Introduction

THE WHOLE IDEA of this book is to take the panic out of Christmas. There's no secret formula contained in these pages, just lots of commonsense ideas, advice and information, as well as dozens of delicious recipes, to help you plan – and enjoy – one of the busiest times of year. This book doesn't forget you've got lots of other things on your mind apart from turkey and mince pies – like shopping, planning parties, choosing gifts, making decorations, not to mention running the home and looking after the family as usual.

For three generations, Good Housekeeping has been helping millions of readers prepare for Christmas, and now you can share in that expertise. Everything is explained in easy-to-follow steps, from making all kinds of decorations for the tree and home to icing the Christmas cake. There is a complete Christmas countdown to take you right through from pudding and mincemeat making in November to serving up the turkey on the big day (vegetarians and those opting for a turkey-free Christmas haven't been forgotten either).

The entertaining chapter is full of inspirational ideas for all kinds of parties – dinners, suppers, buffets and drinks – and each menu has a countdown to tell you exactly what to do when, leaving you the minimum to do on the day. There are lots of hints and ideas for making things go smoothly outside the kitchen too.

Mail order is a growing part of Christmas shopping and at the back of the book you will find a comprehensive list of companies who can supply everything from free-range turkeys to fresh sage for your stuffing.

More than anything, this is the book designed to be your best friend for Christmas: reliable, practical, and lots of fun too.

Christmas Trees

W ITH ITS GLOWING LIGHTS, glittering decorations, delicious pine scent and handsome green foliage, the Christmas tree is one of the best loved symbols of the festive season.

Legend has it that Martin Luther created the first Christmas tree. He was so entranced by the sight of the stars shining through the branches of fir trees in his native Germany that he tried to reproduce the effect by decking out a tree with candles. In Britain, the custom of decorating a tree at Christmas is only about 150 years old; it was started by Prince Albert and Queen Victoria who set up a tree at Windsor Castle for their children.

One of the prettiest sights at Christmas – a traditional fir tree covered with lights and gleaming decorations.

9

CHOOSING A CHRISTMAS TREE

First of all, consider the size of the room the tree will stand in. It's amazing how dwarfed a 2 metre (6 foot) tree can look in a large high hall; similarly how overpowered a small sitting room or hallway can be by a too generous specimen. Don't forget that once mounted the tree might be another 30cm (12 inches) or so higher, while mounting it on table or chest will add yet more height.

The most popular tree sold in the UK is the Norway Spruce. It is the classic triangular shape, fragrant, fairly soft needled, and usually the cheapest type of real tree to buy. Its major drawback is that the needles shed all over the carpet, and impale passing people and pets. There are other varieties that do not shed so readily, such as the Nordmann and Noble firs, but these tend to be more expensive.

The following tips will help you get the most from your tree, whichever kind you choose.

● A British-grown tree will be fresher, and therefore last longer, than an imported specimen. If there is a tree plantation near you, buy from it direct. Otherwise, garden centres and nurseries are usually reliable suppliers.

● Before buying, bounce the tree a few times to check the branches are springy and that the needles aren't falling. Avoid trees with any bald or discoloured branches.

● Most trees are sold cut, without roots. These last better if you saw off the base of the stump and stand the tree in water for a few days before bringing indoors.

● Use an anti-desiccant, available from supermarkets and garden centres, before bringing the tree inside. This helps prevent needle drop and helps to reduce fire risk.

● Indoors, mount your tree in a water holding stand, keeping this topped up regularly. Try not to site the tree near a fire or radiator.

● Container-grown trees can last from Christmas to Christmas, although they obviously get bigger every year. You could start with a small tree from a nursery, planted in a tub. After use, this can be buried in the garden, then lifted out the following year. Once inside you will need to keep the tree well watered.

● Trees grown in a field and then transferred to pots are less likely to survive as the roots are often too damaged from being dug up. That said, a tree may survive to be replanted after Christmas if it is kept well watered indoors in a tub of wet sand or shingle.

For a list of tree plantations around the country, send an SAE to the British Christmas Tree Growers Association, 12 Lauriston Road, London SW19 4TQ (081-946-2695).

GROW YOUR OWN CHRISTMAS TREE

Children will love watching their own tree grow from seed into tiny perfect firs. Start in autumn and by next Christmas you should have a healthy crop.

Buy a packet of suitable seeds such as *Picea breweriana* or *P. abies*.

To get these seeds to grow, you have to make them 'believe' they have been through a cold winter, and that spring has arrived. To do this, mix the seeds with a little damp soil, put them into a polythene bag, seal it tightly and put in the refrigerator for three weeks (NOT the freezer compartment). Then take the seeds out, put them carefully into pots of soil, then cover with a little soil on top. Put the pots into polythene bags to keep in the moisture and put them on a cool windowsill – ie not one directly above a radiator. Soon the first shoots should appear, and by the spring there should be some healthy plants. The pots can then be put outside. Repot as necessary as they grow. By next December they should be perfect miniature trees.

A red and green theme works well on any size of tree. Here, large bows add drama to the colour scheme, while the large baubles catch and reflect the light. A pile of smartly wrapped presents under the tree completes the effect.

CHRISTMAS TREE DECORATIONS

In Britain, about five million Christmas trees are sold every year, and every family has its own way of choosing and putting on the all-important decorations. In recent years, themed trees have become popular, and you and the family can have great fun picking and designing your own theme. Traditionalists may prefer to stick to a twinkling, busy jumble of lights, tinsel, baubles, beads, fruits and nuts, and certainly this looks wonderful on a stately tree in a large room.

But for those wanting to create something more sophisticated, or perhaps tie in with other Christmas decorations, a theme is an excellent idea. Also, for those decorating a tree for the first time it is far easier, and cheaper, to stick to a simple decorative idea than try and fill every branch with contrasting baubles and beads.

TRADITIONAL RED AND GREEN
This never dates and looks classy without being too formal. You don't have to stick to baubles for colour: ribbons tied in lavish bows, artificial fruits, strings of glass or wooden beads, and imaginative home-made decorations (see page 16) can all echo the greens and reds of your scheme.

SNOW WHITE
This is a wonderful idea for a small tree. Use simple white tree lights, then a selection of white and silver ornaments arranged along the branches. Stick to smallish ones to keep in scale with the tree, and create a fairytale, ethereal look.

NAIVE CHARM
Trees don't have to glitter and glow, and working with the natural colour and texture of the foliage rather than swamping it with sparkle and glitter can create a charming and unusual effect. Tiny cones, dried flowers and pretty handmade and decorated biscuits, together with small white candles are all you need (see page 16 for details of how to make some of these).

TOYSHOP
Every child's delight. Buy miniature sized dolls, teddies, houses, rocking horses, animals, even tiny cars and pieces of furniture in glass, wood or any other attractive material. Hang from the branches with brightly coloured strings. If you don't want the toyshop theme for yourself, you could give the children their own small tree and let them decorate it.

Left A tartan theme makes the most here of a small tree. The simple use of bows and red baubles looks stylish.

Above Another example of using a simple theme to great effect on a small tree. Here tiny home-made heart-shaped biscuits tied on with ribbons give the tree a Scandinavian air (see page 18 for how to make the biscuits).

GOLD, FRANKINCENSE AND MYRRH

For a sumptuous, faintly Eastern mood, choose gold baubles, beads and tiny bells. If you can find some gold candles, these will look particularly effective (do read the safety instructions on page 27 if you intend to light them). Frankincense and myrrh are rather rare, but the gifts the Wise Men brought to Jesus can be echoed with tiny parcels covered in gold paper, then tied up with gold braid or thread. Or if you have any tiny, decorative sample bottles of scent in the house, tie fine gold threads around the necks and hang from the tree.

Rich gold brocade scraps can also turn ordinary baubles into something exotic: glue the fabric around the bauble, finish with a gold bow and thread for hanging. You could also try covering shapes of stiff card with fabric, finishing the edges with braid and leaving a loop for hanging.

SCANDINAVIAN-STYLE

This is another simple idea that looks charmingly naive. To create it, stick to seasonal colours of red, white and green. Echo the heart-shaped holes cut into wooden shutters that are a signature of Scandinavian homes with special home-baked biscuits (see recipe on page 22), cut into a heart and then hung from the tree on loops of cotton; finish with a tiny bow of red and green ribbon. Sit the tree in a plain white container – a waste paper bin would do – and, for the final touch, place on a simple wooden chest or table, which can be covered with a simple cotton table cloth, if you want to protect it.

Gold and silver look especially sumptuous against the background of rich green foliage. Try mixing shop-bought and home-made decorations to create your own unique effect.

AN EDIBLE CHRISTMAS TREE

This makes a superb table-top decoration that really does look – and taste – good enough to eat. A cone of Oasis (from florists' and garden centres) is set inside a plant pot, covered in jellied fruits, then finished with a bow.

YOU WILL NEED: Oasis cone, sharp knife, plant pot or dish to hold tree, foil, sticky tape, jellied fruits, cocktail sticks, dressmaking pins, long fronds of ivy, ribbon for bow to finish.

METHOD: Cut down the Oasis cone so the base sits snugly inside the rim of your dish or pot; cover with foil and secure at the back with sticky tape. Next, wind the ivy around the covered cone, keeping in place with the dressmaking pins (insert the pins in a downward direction to make sure no sharp points protrude). Spear the jellied fruits on to wooden cocktail sticks, then plunge them firmly into the cone until it is covered. Finish with a large bow tied around the pot.

Made in smaller sizes, these trees would make attractive individual place setting decorations.

The tree that looks good enough to eat. An Oasis cone is covered with delicious jellied fruits and a silky bow adds the finishing touch. You could make smaller versions of these trees as novel place-setting decorations.

Not all trees need lights to look festive. Here bunches of dried white flowers set off perfectly the scarlet and green of the other decorations. Tartan bows add fullness to the branches and brighten up the table supporting the tree.

TREE DECORATIONS TO MAKE YOURSELF

In *Decorations to Make & Gift Wrapping* there are many beautiful decorations to make for all around the house. Some, like the Victorian cornucopias (page 42) and copper leaves (page 43) would look equally pretty on a tree. And don't forget that piles of prettily-wrapped presents heaped under the branches can create a wonderful extra focus of interest – there are lots of wrapping ideas on page 52. Here are some quick and easy items for decorating your tree: some

take only seconds to make, and older children will love being involved in such festive enterprises. So spread out lots of newspapers and have a go!

DRIED FLOWERS

Bunches of fragrant, dried flowers look and smell wonderful against the background of green scented pine. Try to use flowers with deep, rich colours. Divide them into small bunches, trim the stems to about 7.5cm (3 inches) and wrap each bunch with fuse wire to fix it to the tree. Finish with a bow of wide satin ribbon. Cinnamon sticks can be given a similar treatment.

SPRAYING AND PAINTING

There are many different kinds of paint to choose from today: you will find all kinds of gold and silver paints, inks, powders, sprays, even wax. Gold powder can be particularly subtle: brush on to the clean dry surface of the desired object. Try artists' supplies shops and good stationers for the best selection. When painting or spraying, lay down plenty of newspaper first. Open a window – the fumes can be quite powerful. Don't smoke or have any naked flames nearby – the solvents contained in the products are usually highly inflammable.

BOWS

Best effects are obtained from stiffer ribbons or wide braids as these give better defined loops and tails. Wired ribbons are perfect – very fine wire threaded invisibly up the sides of the ribbon mean the bow can be pulled into a permanent, more flamboyant shape. They are available at most department stores and haberdashers.

NUTS AND CONES

Wired together, these can make charming small garlands. Drill through the nuts (not too large a hole), thread through florists' wire and twist the two ends together to make a stem. Bunch wired nuts in threes and, if required, add pine cones which have been wired around their base with florists' wire. Dried flowers could also be added for extra colour.

Paper hearts

YOU WILL NEED: Paper (plain gift wrap or thin blotting paper) in two colours, ruler, scissors, ribbon, tissue paper, tiny gifts or chocolates.

METHOD: Follow the written and drawn instructions.

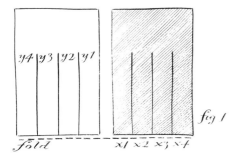

1 Taking the first sheet of paper, fold it (so the colour shows on the outside) and cut out two perfect rectangles (one from each colourway) measuring 30.5 × 10 cm (12 × 4 inches).

2 Fold each rectangle (with colour showing) in half to form a rectangle 15 × 10 cm (6 × 4 inches) and draw lines 2.5 cm (1 inch) apart and about 10.5 cm (4½ inches) away from the folded edge towards the open end. Repeat with the other rectangle. Cut the lines you have drawn. You are now ready to start weaving. (See drawing 1.)

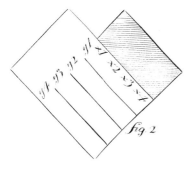

3 Place rectangle Y over rectangle X as shown in drawing 2. Hold the two rectangles in position, lift up all the Y strips and peel back X1. Let the Y strips down again and hold X1 ready to start weaving.

Note: Although the rows of strips look like strips, each one forms a paper loop, and as you weave the strips X and Y, you will in fact be passing each one through a loop.

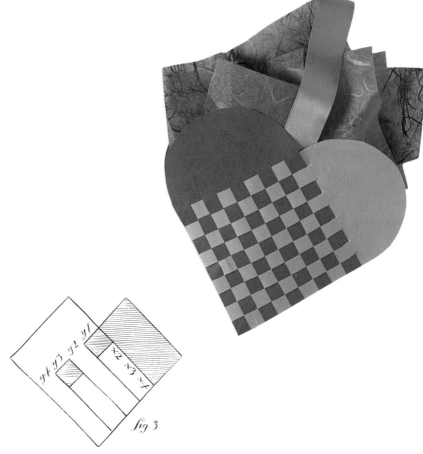

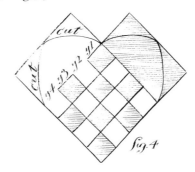

4 Holding strip X1, pass strip Y1 through it; pass strip X1 through Y2; holding strip X1, pass strip Y3 through it; pass strip X1 through Y4 to complete the first row. (See drawing 3.)

5 Weave strip X2 in the same way, but start by passing strip X2 through strip Y1 first, so that the colours are reversed. Straighten the rows so that the pattern looks neat as you work.

6 Repeat with the last two rows. Your weaving is now complete.

7 Cut semicircles at the top, forming the heart shape. (See drawing 4.) To make a loop, attach a piece of ribbon with sticky tape on to the inside of the paper heart. The paper heart bag may be filled with tissue, tiny gifts or chocolates before hanging on the tree.

Once you have mastered the technique of making a paper heart using four strips, you can go on to make hearts with more strips, like the one shown above. To make it, cut strips 1 cm (½ inch) apart. The rectangles remain the same size.

PAPER 'BAUBLE'

Scrunch up a sheet of tissue paper and mould it into a sphere. Cut a piece of ribbon for the hanging loop, about 45cm (18 inches) long, and attach both ends to the base of the ball, using sticky tape. Cut a square of tissue paper, 28cm (11 inch) side measurement, and place the paper ball in the middle. Gather the four corners, making sure the loop is sticking out, then mould the tissue paper around the ball. Keep in place with a ribbon tied in a bow.

CONES

Spray paint the cones. When dry, attach a ribbon for hanging with a safety pin driven through the base of the cone.

PAPER BOWS

Cut a 36cm (14 inch) length of paper ribbon, fold into thirds ie 12cm (5 inches), gather in the middle and tie with string. Cover the string with ribbon and tie to the tree.

ICING HEARTS

Knead together 225g (8oz) ready-to-roll icing with three puffs of peppermint-flavoured denture fixative. (Strange but true, this is the best way to harden the decorations.) Thinly roll out the mixture and stamp out heart shapes using a 5cm (2 inch) heart-shaped cutter. Stamp out small holes for hanging, using the point of a plain 1cm (½ inch) piping nozzle. Leave to dry for 24 hours on a sheet of nonstick parchment. Re-knead the trimmings in a polythene bag, incorporating a few drops of red food colouring. Roll out thinly as before and stamp out a second set of hearts, this time using a 2.5cm (1 inch) cutter. Leave to dry. Sandwich the white and red hearts together with a little royal icing and leave to set for 2-3 hours.

Note: These decorations are not edible.

STRINGS OF BOWS

You will need a 2 metre (6 ft 6 inch) piece of string plus sheets of coloured crepe paper. Cut the paper into pieces about 7.5-10 × 6.5 cm (3-4 × 2½ inches). Pleat into folds like a fan. Tie the string around the middle of each fan, flaring each end out to make a bow shape. Repeat every 6.5 cm (2½ inches) of string.

CURTAIN RING

Wind ribbon around a wooden curtain ring, leaving about 10cm (4 inches) hanging before starting. After covering the ring, knot and tie the ribbon ends. Cut to the required length – a tail of about 10-15cm (4-6 inches) looks attractive – and thread the finished ring on to a branch.

ACORN TASSEL

Paint two wooden light-pull acorns your favourite Christmas colour. When dry, thread ribbon through one acorn and tie a knot. Similarly, thread on the second acorn at the other end of the ribbon. Tie on to branches in a bow.

RAFFIA TASSEL

Fold 28cm (11 inch) loops of raffia into a thick skein. Fold this in half and tie a ribbon securely around the folded skein, about one third along from one end. Cut the loops at the other end. Thread a ribbon through the loops at the top end for hanging.

Above *A string of brightly coloured paper bows is easy to make and looks dramatic.*

Opposite page *A treeful of colour. Most of these decorations are very easy to make, and are most effective massed together so the tree looks very busy and eye-catching.*

EDIBLE CHRISTMAS TREE DECORATIONS

These are more traditional than you might think: when Prince Albert first made Christmas trees popular by importing them to Windsor Castle for the Royal children, they were hung with gingerbread men and cakes. You can revive this tradition easily with the following deliciously edible ideas. Remember to remove the strings before eating!

APRICOT DROPS

Thread a large needle with double thickness thread. Thread together dried apricots, or experiment with mixtures of dried and glacé fruits, knotting one end of the double thread to keep them on it. At the top end, either join the ends of the thread to form a loop, or add a ribbon bow and tie on and knot another length of thread into a loop for hanging.

CHERRIES

Buy glacé cherries with stalks and, using a medium thickness needle, thread a fine gold thread through each fruit. Knot at the bottom and tie on to the tree.

ORANGES AND LEMONS

Using a fine needle and gold thread, gather together crystallised orange and lemon peel into jagged clusters. Tie the ends of the thread together. Add a bow and a loop of thread for hanging.

TINY ORANGES

Make or buy marzipan oranges (use orange food colouring kneaded into almond paste if making your own). Add miniature leaves by colouring a little ready-to-roll icing green and cutting out leaf shapes with a small, sharp knife. Stick two leaves on to each orange with a dot of egg white. Thread a loop of gold braid right through the orange and tie underneath.

BAGS OF GOLD

These are very easy to make. Just cut out rounds of gold or white netting, fill with gold-wrapped chocolate money, gold dragees or nuts, then tie into little bags with gold ribbon. Sugared almonds also look pretty.

CHOCOLATE BARS

Buy small chocolate bullion bars (from your sweet shop or supermarket). Thread and knot a loop of gold braid through the end of each bar for hanging. Alternatively, foil wrapped chocolate mints, also on sale in most supermarkets, can be tied up like tiny parcels with gold thread, then hung from the tree with a loop of thread.

MARZIPAN SWEETS

Thread a loop of gold thread through bought marzipan fruits, taking care not to make too big a hole. Add bows of gold and tartan ribbon.

POPCORN BALLS

Make up some sweet or savoury popcorn, (caramel flavour microwave popcorn is ideal) according to instructions. For sweet popcorn, allow to cool slightly, until it is comfortable to handle. Press into small clusters between the palms of your hands (you will have to press quite hard to make the popcorn stick together). Allow to cool completely. Thread a fine needle with fine gold thread and push carefully through a popcorn cluster. Then gather some thick gold ribbon or fine net and thread on above the cluster, arranging it into neat folds, then add on another popcorn cluster. Knot the thread to form a loop for hanging. Alternatively, just thread one popcorn cluster and top with a gold or tartan bow.

For savoury popcorn, thread each individual piece of popcorn on a long fine gold thread. Either hang or loop on the tree.

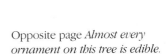

Opposite page Almost every ornament on this tree is edible.

Above and below Bags of gold and gold chocolate bars on a string make delicious seasonal decorations. Tiny oranges and clusters of popcorn take moments to make and are an unusual alternative to baubles and beads.

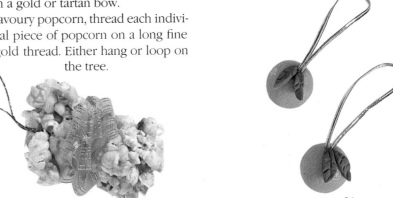

TEDDY BAKES

These look fun on a tree. Use this standard white bread dough – or a packet bread mix – to mould teddy bears and other simple shapes.

15g (½oz) fresh yeast or 7.5ml (1½tsp) dried yeast and pinch sugar
700g (1½lb) strong white flour
10ml (2tsp) salt
knob of lard or white vegetable fat
cloves, currants and sea salt to decorate
beaten egg

1 Crumble the fresh yeast and blend until smooth with about 450ml (¾ pint) tepid water. If using dried yeast, sprinkle it into the water with the sugar and leave in a warm place for 15 minutes until frothy. Mix the flour and salt in a large bowl and rub in the lard. Make a well in the dry ingredients and add the yeast liquid. Stir in with a fork or wooden spoon.
2 Work it to a soft dough using your hand, until it leaves the sides of the bowl clean. Add a little extra water if the mixture is too dry.
3 Turn the dough on to a floured work surface and knead thoroughly for about 10 minutes or until the dough feels firm and elastic and no longer sticky. Shape it into a ball and place in a large oiled mixing bowl. Cover the bowl with a clean tea towel to prevent a skin forming and allow to rise in a warm place until it has doubled in size and springs back when pressed gently with a floured finger.
4 Knock back the dough and turn on to a lightly floured surface. Knead well for 2-3 minutes, flattening it firmly with the knuckles to knock out the air bubbles.

5 Tear off small pieces to shape the teddies, using cloves or currants for eyes, noses, etc. Place on greased baking sheets. Brush with beaten egg and leave to rise for about 15 minutes.
6 Sprinkle with sea salt if wished. Bake at 190°C (375°F) mark 5 for about 15 minutes until golden brown, shiny and sounding hollow when tapped. Cover with foil, reduce the temperature to 170°C (325°F) mark 3 and bake until completely dried out – about 15 minutes. Cool and attach ribbons.

Note: These decorations are not edible.

CHRISTMAS TREE FAVOURS

Store these biscuits in an airtight container and ice them as required.

175g (6oz) softened butter or margarine
125g (4oz) granulated sugar
125g (4oz) soft brown sugar
1 egg
350g (12oz) plain white flour
2.5ml (½tsp) salt
10ml (2tsp) ground cinnamon
1 egg white
sifted icing sugar
food colourings

1 Beat the butter with the granulated sugar and brown sugar in a bowl until fluffy.

Gradually beat in the egg. Sift the flour, salt and cinnamon and fold into the butter mixture; beat well. Press into a ball and if necessary chill for 30 minutes.

2 Roll out the biscuit mixture on a floured work surface to about 0.5cm (¼ inch) thick and cut out Christmas shapes. Make small holes for ribbons for hanging.

3 Lift the favours on to baking sheets and prick them lightly with a fork. Bake at 180°C (350°F) mark 4 for about 15 minutes or until well browned and firm to the touch. Cool slightly on the sheets, then on a wire rack.

4 To make the icing, beat the egg white until frothy and gradually add enough sifted icing sugar to make a stiff coating or piping consistency.

5 Colour the icing and pipe patterns over the biscuits.

TO FREEZE:
Pack, uniced, in layers and freeze.

TO USE:
Thaw at room temperature for about 1 hour.
MAKES ABOUT 20-24

Christmas tree favours, spicy biscuits in seasonal shapes piped with icing patterns, look delightful hung from branches with thick red braid.

SPICE COOKIES

Cut these cookies into all kinds of Christmassy shapes – stars, trees, snowmen – and add holes with a skewer so the cookies can be threaded with ribbon and hung from a tree. The iced and sponged variations look particularly effective against the greenery, as well as tasting delicious. These cookies would make a perfect gift if you are a house guest somewhere.

100g (4oz) plain white flour
2.5ml (½tsp) ground mixed spice
5ml (1 tsp) ground ginger
pinch baking powder
65g (2½oz) butter or margarine
50g (2oz) light muscovado sugar
15ml (1tbsp) milk
10ml (2tsp) orange juice

1 Mix the flour, spices and baking powder together in a bowl. Rub in the butter. In a small saucepan gently heat the sugar and milk until well blended. Cool. Stir into the dry ingredients with the orange juice. Work together to form a smooth dough. Chill for 15 minutes.

2 Turn out on to a lightly floured work surface and roll out to 0.5cm (¼ inch) thick. Stamp out shapes using biscuit cutters, about 6.5cm (2½ inch) in size, such as trees, stars, etc. Place on baking sheets and make holes with a skewer to take a piece of ribbon after baking to hang the biscuits on the tree. Bake at 180°C (350°F) mark 4 for 12-15 minutes or until golden brown. Cool on a wire rack. Store in an airtight tin for up to a week.

TO FREEZE:
Pack in layers and freeze.

TO USE:
Thaw at room temperature for about 1 hour.
MAKES 12-15

VARIATIONS
ICED COOKIES On a surface dusted with icing sugar, roll out thinly some ready-to-use icing. Using the same biscuit cutters as for Spice Cookies, stamp out the same shapes as the biscuits. Brush the cooked biscuit tops with warm apricot jam and press on the icing shapes. Press a skewer through the icing to re-form the hole, then leave for 10 minutes to dry. Thread ribbons carefully through the holes.
SPONGED COOKIES Beat 125g (4oz) icing sugar with 1 egg white. Divide between two or three small bowls and add a few drops of food colouring to each one, such as red, green, etc. Dip a piece of damp natural sponge into the coloured icing and dab over Iced Cookies to form a sponged pattern. Leave to dry for about 20 minutes. You can also stencil the biscuits in this way using cardboard templates of shapes.

Here, blue and gold create a sophisticated tree that looks especially dramatic against a blue background. Gold cones and candles create hundreds of gleaming surfaces, while simple metallic blue baubles complete the effect.

CHRISTMAS LIGHTS

With so many designs to choose from, it can be hard deciding which lights to buy. The plain white bulbs that have become so popular in recent years are perfect if you are planning dramatic tree decorations that would clash with more flamboyantly designed lights. On the other hand, illuminated lanterns, flowers, baubles, snowflakes, star and candle shapes look extremely pretty and festive, and can suggest an immediate theme for the rest of your decorations.

As a rough guide, you will need to buy twenty lights for a tree of up to 1.6 metres (5 foot). Over this you will require one or more sets of thirty-five or forty lights.

SWITCHING ON

The plug to the lights should have a 3 amp fuse fitted. When replacing one of the lamps (and this should be done as soon as one goes, even if the rest of the lamps stay illuminated) you must use 12V bulbs for sets of twenty lights, 7.2V for sets of thirty-five, and 6V for sets of forty.

Always check the lights work a couple of weeks before you plan to buy your tree and again before arranging them on the tree. Then you have time to sort out faulty lights.

If you have a lot of different decorations competing for attention, as here with this toyshop theme, it is best to choose simple lights which do not fight them. The plain bulbs shown here are ideal.

IF THE LIGHTS DON'T WORK: Check one of the bulbs hasn't worked loose. Unplug, then push or screw each bulb gently but firmly into each socket before trying again. If there is still not a glimmer, check the fuse lamp (usually tipped white) is working by either using a battery (which will illuminate it if working) or a bulb tester. Work through the other lamps in the same way. Replace any faulty ones, but only replace the fuse lamp with a similar bulb as it protects the whole set from overloading.

CANDLES

These are pretty but very hazardous. If you are determined to use them, take the following precautions to minimise the risks:

● Make sure the candles are not directly below a branch, and that the whole tree is well away from curtains, furniture, cards, and anything else inflammable.
● Keep a fire extinguisher or bucket of water to hand in case of emergency.
● Never leave the room when the candles are lit.
● Check the candles are absolutely upright before lighting, and that candleholders are securely fastened to the branches.
● Use a fire-retardant spray on foliage before decorating the tree.

Decorating Your Home

'DECK THE HALLS WITH boughs of holly' carol the singers as Christmas approaches. In ancient times, pagans revered evergreens such as holly, ivy, mistletoe, pine and spruce as symbols of continuing life in the depths of winter. Today we appreciate them for their fresh scent, glowing colours and ability to transform the most ordinary room. There is some-thing about the combination of glossy evergreen foliage, brilliant berries, warm candlelight, bowls of gleaming fruits, baskets of nuts and cones that captures the full splendour of the season.

Decorating your home for Christmas can be as simple or as elaborate a task as you choose, but the warm glow of candles will always be welcome.

29

With so many shops now selling all kinds of greenery you won't be limited just to holly, ivy and trimmings from your tree. Bay, eucalyptus, box, yew and herbs like rosemary and thyme look and smell wonderful. Some of the fake evergreens are now so good, it is hard to spot them – spruce garlands, ivy fronds and tiny pine trees can all be draped and arranged to look like the real thing – and of course used year after year.

When planning a decorating scheme, take into account the size and proportions of the room as well as the background colour scheme. A low ceilinged room will only feel more closed in if heavy swags of greenery are hung around door frames and along picture tops. Keep decorations at eye level or lower to create the illusion of greater height. Similarly, a huge room can obviously take bigger, bolder schemes, and you can have fun creating separate areas of decorative interest around the room – on tables, along shelves and mantelpieces, over pictures and fireplaces.

And, of course, the scene of all the action on Christmas Day, the dining table, deserves special attention too. Now is the time to bring out the best china and glasses – perhaps adding in one or two pieces with a Christmas theme: if you like the effect you could start collecting and add more each year. A table centrepiece looks marvellous, and needn't be elaborate or hard to make – a simple pyramid of fruits such as tangerines, glossy red apples or gleaming grapes looks stunning draped with ivy and set in a glass bowl or arranged on a polished metal stand. Or perhaps you have a ready-made centrepiece – a beautiful gilt candelabra, gilded ornament or wonderfully painted vase or bowl – that deserves the limelight. Fruit, flowers, candles and pretty bows and baubles can all transform these pieces into something stunning.

Even if space is tight at the table, making sure all the glass, china and linen is absolutely spotless and gleaming will create the right backdrop for your splendid food. Small touches like colourful ribbons around napkins, a red or green tablecloth, and a couple of tiny seasonal flower arrangements that can be easily moved from the table before the turkey is served, will look very pretty and not at all out of scale.

Simple but effective – candles create pools of light on the table, and along a shelf and mantelpiece.

THEMES FOR ROOMS

Here are a variety of suggestions for decorative schemes for rooms.

CLASSIC RED AND GREEN

Greenery, berries, baubles, bows and candles pick up the colour scheme. Try garlanding doorways (see page 47 for instructions to make), pictures and shelves with evergreens, then add red candles, Christmas cards hung on to broad green ribbons, a red cloth for the dining table and a gleaming display of fruits and nuts entwined with ivy to create a classical seasonal setting.

BAROQUE

Gold is the key to this theme. Build around a golden or gilt centrepiece – it doesn't have to be an heirloom, it could be a statuette, candelabra or candlesticks, even a small bust or cherub's head. Picking up the gold theme from this, you can then add tiny gold baubles nestling in rich greenery, gold braid and ribbon for hanging decorations and cards, flowers arranged in gold bowls and vases, nuts and cones sprayed gold and arranged in baskets, or simply scattered on polished wood or glass surfaces. Offset the richness with touches of green or red, even blue or black. And illuminate everything with tiny candles set in pretty holders – try metal petit-four cases, frosted glasses or splash out on some sconces and make a brilliant light show on a wall.

TARTAN

This always looks warm and welcoming, and is very easy to achieve. Set the scene with a tartan rug thrown over a sofa. Add flamboyant tartan bows to evergreens garlanded around the room and, if you like, pin tartan ribbons to the wall, topped and tailed with bows, for Christmas cards. If you are feeling extravagant, buy some tartan cushions and a couple of tartan lampshades to add the finishing touch.

Complement the rich tones of this scheme with dried flowers, and wicker baskets of nuts and cones nestling in greenery.

Pick out the dominant colour of the tartan you use with candles placed around the room.

WINTER WHITE

The keynotes here are lots of sparkling glass, white candles, fresh flowers and foliage, and subtle touches of colour. The overall effect will be fresh rather than cosy but for those with perhaps limited space who want to avoid being overwhelmed, this decorative scheme is ideal – and very simple to achieve. White candles of varying heights and thicknesses can be placed around the room in strategic places. Try in front of a mirror, on top of glass shelves and polished tabletops (watch for dripping wax though) – anywhere likely to catch and throw back light and reflections. Stick to simple candle-holders – appropriately sized glasses make excellent makeshift holders, or buy them in simple white or pale colours – they needn't cost very much.

Having arranged your candles, you can now think about adding subtle touches of colour, and introducing more reflective surfaces. Experiment with arrangements of pretty foil-wrapped sweets, dishes of pastel or silver-coloured baubles, tiny decorated tins, pretty fake parcels, even decorated small dishes or plates. Attractive by day, they will look stunning lit by flickering candlelight at night.

For the final touch to the room, add touches of greenery – artificial spruce garlanded around a mirror adds a touch of drama. You could pile up seasonal fruits such as pumpkins, or any large fruit like melons, in front of it for the final effect. Bowls of flower bulbs forced for Christmas or pale vases of creamy flowers will create pools of colour around the room. And what about a pile of beautifully wrapped presents piled on to a plain shelf or table to make a charming decorative feature?

Left *Tartan always looks warm and welcoming – dried flowers and cones make a good contrast to the richness of the colours. Tartan wrapping paper tied with plain or tartan ribbon turns simple parcels into a smart decorative idea.*

33

MORE DECORATIVE IDEAS

Once you have your main decorations in place and the tree erected, you might like to create a few specially festive corners about the room or rest of the house. A small table, a windowsill, a set of shelves or corner cupboard, a fireplace can all be brought into festive focus with a few clever touches.

A small table, covered with a deep red cloth, makes a delightful resting place for a traditional wicker or twig basket filled with berries, lush foliage, cinnamon sticks (for fragrance) and carefully arranged nightlights. If your hallway is small, this is a particularly easy way of making it feel warm and welcoming.

A side table, pushed against a wall, can be given a similar treatment, but try pinning cards behind it, if you don't mind the small pin holes afterwards, to create a colourful backdrop.

A SIMPLE TABLE ARRANGEMENT

Make use of a small, deep window to display a wonderful arrangement of Christmassy fruits, flowers and foliage.

YOU WILL NEED: A wicker basket, a block of Oasis (available from florists), florists' wire, scissors, clippers or secateurs, a plastic tub such as a large size yogurt or ice cream container, a polythene bag, and a brass pot or cache pot that fits inside the wicker basket. Greentack (the florists' equivalent of Blutack) is useful, but not essential. You will also need a base hook to prevent the Oasis from floating in the container.

METHOD: Line the brass pot or cachepot with the polythene bag to protect it. Put the Oasis inside the plastic container, making sure the Oasis sits above the rim to enable you to fix stems at an angle for a trailing effect. Put the container and Oasis into the brass pot, and place these into the centre of the wicker basket. Snip off and trim lengths of different greenery: spruce, blue pine, eucalyptus and ivy offer lots of contrast and tend to last longer than ordinary Christmas tree pine. Cover the Oasis with greenery,

building up and out until you have the required shape. Next add the fruit, wrapped in ribbon like parcels, and then attached to florists' wire, and finally cones, bows and some small silver beads – avoid large baubles, which would be too dominant.

CHRISTMAS PLANTS

These add welcome colour in the depths of winter, but need extra loving care if they are to survive in dry, centrally heated homes. Cinerarias, azaleas, cyclamen and primulas cannot look their best in a hot desiccated atmosphere, so make sure they are placed well away from radiators. Mist them frequently, or stand in shallow pots containing pebbles which you keep moist. Alternatively, place a saucer of water near them: as the water evaporates, it creates a moist microclimate to help the plant thrive.

BULBS: November is the time to bring your forced bulbs indoors to get them ready for Christmas flowering. If you have a number of pots, leave a few of them in a cool room or the greenhouse to delay flowering a little and give a display spread over several weeks instead of just one or two. Tie a ribbon around the bowls for an extra festive touch.

MINI CHRISTMAS TREES

These look delightful on the Christmas lunch table, or massed together on a table top or shelf. Buy miniature cupressus trees, such as *Chamaecyparis lawsoniana* Ellwood's Gold, from your local garden centre. Plant into small pots or arrange several into a terracotta trough, then tie on tiny baubles, bows and other miniature decorations. Once the festive season is over, the trees can be planted out in the garden to give all year round pleasure.

TABLE SWAGS

This is a simple way of transforming a small side table.

YOU WILL NEED: Enough cream fabric to cover the table and provide several 18cm (7 inch) wide strips of material, lengths of ivy, real or fake.

METHOD: Cover the table with the material, hemming raw edges that show. Cut 18cm (7 inch) strips of the extra fabric on the bias and wind each strip along the length of the ivy, allowing the leaves to protrude through, to create swags. Pin these around the sides of the table.

fresh ones as they die. To keep your artificial flowers and foliage in top condition, wash them in a dilute solution of good quality washing up liquid, rinse gently in plain water, then hang upside down to dry. Or follow the manufacturers' care instructions for guidance.

Tiny Christmas trees decked out in miniature baubles and bows make a very pretty decoration for any table top or shelf. Look out for miniature cupressus trees at your local garden centre or nursery.

FLOWERS

Apart from bulbs and cut flowers, consider investing in some top quality silk blooms and foliage which will last from year to year. A mixture of real and fake can look particularly attractive: try combining silk lilies and old roses with real foliage, or fake foliage massed around real apples or tangerines. You could even mix real and fake flowers together in the same display, replacing the

LIGHT SHOWS

Invest in several pretty sconces or candle holders suitable for attaching to the wall. Then experiment with designs: try arranging them as a pyramid – to echo a Christmas tree shape, or in a circle or star. Add candles, and you have the perfect light show for your room.

35

TABLE SETTINGS

Christmas is the time when people and food come together a great many times in a few days: for the Christmas meal itself, parties, buffets, family suppers, dinner parties, teas and so on. Wonderful food deserves a wonderful setting, and a little care spent laying and decorating a table for a meal will give you, your family and guests extra pleasure at mealtimes.

The keynotes of any successful table setting, as said earlier, are scrupulously clean glassware and cutlery that shines, crisp linen and, where possible, china that enhances the appearance of the food – for example, blue plates as a rule do nothing for white meats like turkey.

FORMAL SETTING (5 COURSES)

The rule for formal settings is to start from the outside and work in, so the cutlery for the first course is on the outside. Cutlery should be set close together.

INFORMAL SETTING (3 COURSES)

Cutlery for the first and main courses is placed on the outside, as for formal settings. Dessert cutlery is set above the place mat; butter knife is on the side plate.

ELEGANT NAPKIN

A pretty folded napkin is easier to make than it looks. First, fold the napkin in half diagonally, then bring the left and right-hand corners up to meet at the apex (drawing 1).

Turn the napkin over, and fold the lower corner up slightly (drawing 2).

Fold the left and right-hand corners underneath the napkin on a slight diagonal, pressing folds lightly in place (drawing 3).

The napkin is ready to lay on a plate (drawing 4).

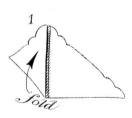

These are the basics then. You can build up a theme using a few very simple ideas.

SILVER AND WHITE

Gleaming glass, silver and silver-coloured cutlery and table accessories, with pure white linen, create one of the simplest and most elegant table settings.

Don't worry if you do not possess an imposing collection of lead crystal and cut glass. Cheaper moulded and pressed glass looks just as pretty, and you will be far more relaxed about possible breakages!

Tie up white linen (or starched cotton) napkins with a pretty ribbon, perhaps decorated with a few sprigs of dried flowers or a frond of evergreen. Wire on a couple of tiny cones or nuts for the finishing touch. Or, fold the napkins into a pretty shape (see opposite for instructions). For this table setting it is best to stick to plain and discreetly patterned china, and leave the drama to the silverware. For the finishing touch, add white candles in silver holders, with a stunning flower and foliage centrepiece.

Sparkling glass and silverware make a thousand reflections to create a spectacular table setting. Candles and simple white china complete the picture.

FLORAL TABLE CENTREPIECE

This arrangement uses only three kinds of foliage – each with contrasting leaf shapes, and one with berries, and one kind of flower.

YOU WILL NEED: An oval tin or other water-tight container (a silver-coloured fluted loaf tin is ideal); a block of Oasis, waterproof tape, strong scissors or proper florists' scissors, foliage and flowers – it is best to keep these simple.

METHOD: Cut the Oasis to fit the container and stand slightly above the sides. Fix in place with tape attached to the edge of the container. Start with small sprigs of the foliage that will form the body of the arrangement, and push them into the Oasis at random to make a fairly even shape when viewed from all sides. Do not pack the sprigs too densely, leave gaps for the sprigs of the other two types of foliage. Finally dot the flowers around the arrangement, pushing the short stems into the Oasis. Water the Oasis until it is soaked.

Three kinds of foliage in this floral table centrepiece make for contrast and interest. Try and choose specimens with different leaf shapes, one bearing berries, another flowers. Make sure you have enough to cover the Oasis generously.

VICTORIAN OPULENCE

This table setting theme makes striking use of colour. Reds and greens are there, but so too are rich purple and a vivid display of fruits. Try using coloured instead of plain glasses for extra impact, and perhaps small gold-coloured dishes for sauces and delicious accompaniments. Candles add a wonderful glow to the rich colours, and a plain background such as a cotton ticking tablecloth makes sure the overall effect isn't too overwhelming. Add extra touches of colour to napkins with red ribbons around the middle, and a few fronds of rich green ivy twisted around the fruit display.

SIMPLE IVY AND FRUIT CENTREPIECE

Use various fruits of your choice for this table arrangement.

YOU WILL NEED: A wire basket, sphagnum moss to line it, red gloss paint, ivy, various fruits.

METHOD: Paint the basket red, then allow to dry. Fill with damp moss, twine ivy through wires until the moss is concealed, then fill the basket with different fruits.

CHRISTMAS TABLECLOTH

A stencilled cloth makes an unusual background to the meal, and is surprisingly easy to make.

YOU WILL NEED: Enough plain fabric, such as sheeting, to cover your dining table, with allowances for a hem all around, stencils (available from craft shops, or see Suppliers for stockists) – choose seasonal shapes like stars, leaves of holly and ivy, trees, etc. stencil paints, paint brush.

METHOD: Hold the stencil flat to the surface of the fabric. Apply the paint with a light stippling motion, using very little colour on an almost dry brush (rub the excess paint off the brush on to absorbent kitchen paper). Build up deeper tones of colour in several layers. When the stencilling is dry, press with a cool iron to set the design. Finally hem around the cloth for a neat finish.

Decorations to Make & Gift Wrapping

Shop-bought decorations can be very expensive, and you cannot always find what you want. Yet there are dozens of beautiful Christmas ideas you can make yourself, at very little cost, and often with very little effort. The extra bonus is the glow of satisfaction from seeing the results of your work.

Don't worry if you are not a DIY enthusiast, crafts devotee or sewing expert. Many of the ideas described in this chapter are simple enough for quite young children to help with, while some of the more time-consuming and skilled projects, like the wreaths on page 48, will reward your efforts with their individual charm.

Natural materials such as raffia, hessian, muslin and even string can make stunning alternatives to the usual sparkle and glitter of Christmas gift wrappings.

DECORATIONS TO MAKE

Before embarking on making any of the items here, it is a good idea to lay out everything you need first. That way you have everything to hand and aren't scrabbling for vital glue or paint at an awkward moment. Also, at this time of year it is easy to run out of supplies like sticky tape, and infuriating only to find this out in the middle of operations. Lay down lots of newspaper if the project looks messy (and certainly if children are helping!), then read through the instructions twice before starting. If you know you will have to break off in the middle, plan to do so at a convenient point, such as when paint or glue needs to dry.

MINIATURE HOUSES

These look pretty ranged along a shelf, window ledge or mantelpiece. The beauty of them is that the more naive they look the better: painstaking artistry is not necessary. Older children may enjoy making them as an alternative to Christmas cards.

YOU WILL NEED: Light card (reverse sides of cereal box cardboard is perfect), corrugated cardboard, poster or powder paints.

METHOD: Make a basic house shape from the light card. You may prefer to make a template first for the back, front and side walls. If so, use a thicker piece of card to make the drawing out easier. Join the walls together on the inside using sticky tape. Add a roof of corrugated paper, stuck on with light glue or gum. Cut out windows, doors and shutters, then paint. If you like, stick on beads, buttons, tiny dried flowers and straw for decorative detail.

TAPESTRY TABLECLOTH

The rich colours and gleaming threads of this cloth create a wonderful background for festive food and drink.

YOU WILL NEED: A damask tablecloth with a pale jacquard weave – pick one with a central or border design of fruit or flowers (or a Christmas design if you prefer); yarns – either 3 ply wool yarn or stranded cotton, used double; crewel needle, embroidery hoop, a pair of small sharp scissors.

METHOD: Using the hoop and a single thread, outline the shape in stem stitch. Use double thread to fill in each shape in satin stitch or long and short stitches. Shade leaves and petals in tones of the same colour.

VICTORIAN CORNUCOPIAS

These look very pretty filled with dried flowers or simply left empty and arranged in clusters on a table.

YOU WILL NEED: Manila paper, paper glue, patterned paper or fabric decorations such as ribbon, braid, cord, or motifs cut from sprayed or painted paper doilies.

METHOD: Draw a quarter circle segment on the Manila paper. The straight sides should measure about 15cm (6 inches); add 0.5cm (¼ inch) overlap to one of the straight sides, then cut out. Cut out two matching shapes in the decorative paper or fabric and glue to each side of the Manila paper. Glue along overlap on one side, then wrap around the whole piece to form a cone. When dry, trim with your chosen decorations. If you wish, attach a loop for hanging.

CHRISTMAS TOPIARY

This is not actually cutting trees into star or tree shapes, but the effect is similar – and charming. By training indoor plants to grow over sculpted shapes, you can have some wonderful fresh green decorations to brighten up a table, or to give your garden room or conservatory a Christmas mood.

YOU WILL NEED: Oasis (available from florists', garden shops, some department stores), a sharp knife, well grown trailing plants in pots large enough to take an Oasis shape.

METHOD: Cut your desired shape from the Oasis with the knife. Place the shape into the pot of one or more trailing plants (small leaved ivies, tiny *Ficus pumila*, sweet scented jasmine and passionflower are perfect). Peg the stems into place using fine, small hairpins as staples. If you use adult plants, you should be able to cover the shape immediately. Prune from time to time to encourage neat, dense cover.

COPPER LEAVES

These look very pretty scattered around the Christmas dining table, or on any glowing wood surface lit with candles. They are suprisingly easy to make and, of course, will last from year to year.

YOU WILL NEED: A small sheet of copper (or brass if you prefer a more golden colour) available from model shops; sharp scissors, small hammer, spike, such as a knitting needle.

METHOD: Cut out simple leaf shapes: if you like a battered effect, use the small hammer to make tiny dents all over. Add veins by scoring the metal with a spike. If liked, glue on some small coloured marbles with strong adhesive, to look like berries.

THREE WOODEN WISE MEN

These are fun to look at and easy to make.

YOU WILL NEED: Three wooden jointed artists' models about 30cm (12 inches) high – available from artists' supply shops, craft shops and some department stores; scraps of fabric, fuse wire, sticky tape, cardboard, gold paint, gold piping cord.

METHOD: Make capes from the fabric scraps, trimming with gold braid or similar if you like. Fix fuse wire around the underside of the outer edge of each cloak with the sticky tape for a stiffened effect. Then attach capes to the body with gold piping or cord, stiffened with fuse wire. Make crowns and presents from cardboard, then either paint them gold, or cover with fabric and trims.

Covered hatboxes make perfect holders for any awkward-shaped gift. Pretty to look at and easy to make, they are nice enough to give as presents on their own.

CRACKERS

These are always popular. They date back to the 1840s when Tom Smith, a London confectioner, copied the idea of wrapping sweets in coloured twisted paper from the Parisians. He refined and embellished the idea, adding snaps, mottoes and jokes as well as tiny gifts.

Crackers are actually very easy to make yourself, and you can have fun personalising them for Christmas guests, or designing them to complement your other festive decorative schemes. Miniature crackers filled with sweets make perfect stocking fillers for children, or look very pretty hanging from the tree. For adults, what could be nicer than finding your cracker contains a wonderful Christmas present – a set of cuff links or gold chain perhaps?

FOR EACH CRACKER YOU WILL NEED: A rectangle of coloured paper 45 × 18 cm (18 × 7 inches), three rectangles of thin white card 10 × 18 cm (4 × 7 inches), gifts, snaps (see Suppliers for stockists) coloured cord, scissors, double-sided tape, pencil, ruler, decorative ribbon and foliage.

METHOD: Place the rectangles of card on the wrong side of the coloured paper 4cm (1½ inches) in from the short edges and with 4cm (1½ inch) gaps between them. Fix in place with double sided tape (picture 1).

Place the gift and snap along the centre of the card and roll up around them to form a tube about 5cm (2 inches) in diameter (picture 2).

Wind cord around the tube 15cm (6 inches) in from each end and pull gently to gather in, being careful not to tear the paper (picture 3). Tie the cord to hold in the gathers. Fold the 4 cm (1½ inch) overlaps at each end of the cracker to the inside. Decorate the crackers with cardboard shapes, ribbons and dried foliage, then trim the ends with crowns of gold paper if wished.

Arrange in a pretty, paper-lined box.

You can easily personalise your own crackers by adding your choice of decorations. Here, dried flowers, leaves, a tiny ivy frond, and stars and a bow make this box of homemade crackers look especially tantalising. Experiment with your own ideas – stencils, beads, tinsel, or tiny cones and nuts painted silver and gold all look pretty.

DRIED-FLOWER POMANDER

These look very pretty scattered around a room, and would make perfect small Christmas presents.

YOU WILL NEED: A selection of dried flowers on firm stems, including small rosebuds; Oasis, sharp knife.

METHOD: Cut the stems to 2cm (¾ inch), being careful not to damage them. Either buy or carve out a 7cm (2¾ inch) diameter Oasis ball for the base, push the rosebuds in up to the flowerheads, spacing them evenly. Fill in the gaps with the other flowers, packing them close together until the entire surface is covered.

APPLE DOOR FAN

Fresh fruits at Christmas look and smell wonderful. In *Decorating your Home* various fruit arrangements were described for the table, but here is a wonderful bold idea for brightening up any room.

YOU WILL NEED: Thick plywood or blockboard, 5cm (2 inch) nails, apples, some large strong glossy leaves such as laurel, branches of box tree, strong glue, picture hooks for hanging.

METHOD: Measure the width of the door you wish to decorate, then draw a shallow hemisphere shape to this width on to your chosen wood. (Make sure the depth of the hemisphere is not too great to fit between the top of the door frame and the ceiling.) Cut out the shape, hammer the nails through at wide enough intervals to spear through the centre of each apple. Glue on a background of dark, glossy leaves and branches of box. Put on apples when the glue has dried. Hang your fan above the door using strong picture hooks.

Below *This dried flower pomander smells as good as it looks, and is very easy to make.*

Right *A simple garland of evergreen around this mirror looks dramatic.*

GARLANDS

These look beautiful draped around window and door frames, or looped across a mantelpiece. And they don't have to be just an indoor decoration; like wreaths (see page 48) garlands look pretty and welcoming hung outside, around doors and windows. Making a garland is time-consuming but not difficult. You can make them as long or as short as you wish, and ring the changes using different combinations of foliage and decorations.

YOU WILL NEED: A selection of evergreen foliage, length of lightweight rope, about 1cm (⅓ inch) diameter; green gardening string, rubber gloves to protect hands (not essential), trimmings for finished garland.

METHOD: Measure the area you wish to garland. Cut the rope to this length but add on enough to make loops at each end for hanging. Tie the loops with non-slip knots first. Cut your chosen foliage (see page 48 for suggestions) into 20cm (8 inch) lengths. Starting at one end so that you cover the loop, bind about five lengths of evergreen on to the rope with the gardening string, making sure they all lie in the same direction. Work along the length of the rope until it is all densely covered. There should be no rope or string showing, and the garland should end up looking full and generous. To decorate, wire or glue on small nuts, pine cones or glass decorations, or tie on bows. Make sure you hang the garland securely from hooks or nails – they can be heavy. Mist from time to time with a plant spray to keep it looking fresh. An anti-desiccant spray may help stop needle drop – use before you start weaving.

You needn't stick to holly, ivy, and trimmings from your tree to make a wreath. Here, heathers, dried flowers, and eucalyptus create a wonderful contrast of colours and textures. The red bow has fine wires along its edges so it can be pulled into a more flamboyant bow.

WREATHS

These are a delightful way to brighten up a front door at Christmas and make your home instantly welcoming to visitors. Indoors too, wreaths make versatile decorations: they can be dressed up with candles, baubles, ribbons and tiny ornaments, or left plain, with perhaps just a few berries, fruits, cones and fresh or dried flowers for colour and contrast. Miniature wreaths make delightful table decorations, while a circle of evergreen around your turkey centrepiece or Boxing Day ham will add a touch of drama to the meal.

BASIC WREATH KIT
Wreaths are actually quite simple to make and need very little special equipment. The basic kit is: wire cutter pliers, strong scissors or secateurs, several different grades of wire – covered florists' wire is best; fine rubber gloves to protect your hands, a wreath frame from florists' shops or garden centres, sphagnum moss (available from the same outlets) to bind over the frame as a base. Finally, your choice of foliage – a mixture looks more interesting than just one type. Some suitable foliage for wreaths are

holly, ivy, bay, yew, laurel, fir, privet, also herbs such as sage, rosemary and thyme. Obviously choose the glossiest, brightest specimens, and try and give them a drink before using. Cut the bottoms off the stems and leave in water for several hours. Wipe over any dusty leaves and berries with a damp cloth. Spraying your finished wreath with water will help to keep it looking fresh.

CLASSIC CHRISTMAS WREATH
This is a glorious mixture of ivy, holly and spruce with glossy fruits and delicate seedheads added for decoration. Firm fruits are best – limes, lemons and small oranges – because they last longer and their tough skins don't easily bruise. You could use softer fruits like lychees (shown here) which have a wonderful colour and texture, but these are fragile and need careful handling.

As well as the basic wreath kit (see left) which should include a 40cm (16 inch) diameter wreath frame, you will need mossing wire, several 30cm (12 inch) stub wires, your chosen fruits and foliage, thin card, and 1 metre (1 yard) of broad satin or taffeta ribbon.

1 Soak the moss, squeeze out excess water, then bind on to the surface of the wreath frame with mossing wire until it is completely covered. Twist the wire around the frame to attach it at the beginning and end.

4 To wire cones, wrap stub wire around base and twist the ends together. For apples, lemon and limes, push two stub wires at right angles to each other through the base of the fruit; twist the ends together.

2 Cut the foliage into small sprigs and group three stems together to make small bunches. Twist a stub wire around the stems to hold them together, leaving a long length of wire.

5 Arrange fruits in groups and push wires through foliage and moss. Bend ends back into underside of ring and trim. Make bundles of cinnamon with wire. Wrap cord around and knot. Leave one length of wire to attach.

3 Arrange the different foliage in dense groups all lying in one direction and push the wires vertically through the moss to hold in place. Bend the ends back into the underside of the ring and cut off the excess.

6 Fold the ribbon 18cm (7 inches) from one end and pinch the two layers together to form a loop 9cm (3½ inches) long. Make three more 9cm (3½ inch) loops, gathering at this central point, and secure at centre with stub wire, leaving enough wire to fix the rosette. Cut off remaining ribbon and loop over centre to conceal wire. Secure, leaving two ends.

Tip

If you cannot find a florists' wreath, improvise one from chicken wire.

Cut some chicken wire with wire cutters into a rectangle as long as the circumference of the desired wreath, and 30cm (12 inch) wide. Soak sphagnum moss in water, then squeeze out excess moisture. Place the moss down the centre of the wire to form a thick sausage shape. Roll the chicken wire around it to form a tube.

Fix the long edges in place by twisting the ends of the wires and pushing them back into the moss. Bring both ends of the tube together to form a ring and 'stitch' them together with mossing wire.

HEART-SHAPED WREATH

A charming variation on the circular wreath, this is perfect for hanging on the front door or in the porch. The mixture of ivy, berries and fresh herbs used means it smells as good as it looks.

YOU WILL NEED: Basic wreath kit (see page 48), lengths of ivy, berries such as holly, skimmia or even rose hips, fresh herbs such as thyme, sage and rosemary.

METHOD: Bend the florists' wire wreath into a heart shape. Bind handfuls of sphagnum moss on to the frame with florists' wire. Arrange the foliage in small bunches all over, pushing the stems firmly into the moss. Hold the larger bunches in place with short lengths of wire pushed through the moss to the wrong side. Make sure the leaves of the foliage point in the same direction, and are closely packed so they overlap and completely hide the moss base.

A CHRISTMAS CRIB

Nativity cribs are a very old part of the Christmas ritual. They evolved as a simple way of bringing the story of the birth of Jesus to everyone, and while once they were designed for public display, today many homes, especially in Italy and Spain, have their own.

Cribs are fun to make, and needn't be elaborate. You can leave the figures plain, or add detail with paints, fabrics, beads and trimmings.

FOR THE CRIB

YOU WILL NEED: Thin card for the figures, thicker cardboard for the stable, paints, glue, fabrics, cotton wool, trimmings for gowns etc, string or wool, wooden skewers, sticky tape, white tissue paper, black felt-tip pen, gummed paper shapes, raffia or straw.

STANDING FIGURES Following the basic shapes in the photograph, draw the outline of each figure in pencil on a thin card or an empty cereal box. Allow for a 5cm (2 inch) deep flap at the base as a hinged support for the figure; score a line to mark this. Cut out the shapes and fold the flaps back.

MARY AND BABY JESUS Paint the faces of Mary and Jesus, then paint Mary's blue robe (Plaka paints from art shops are ideal). You will need to allow time for the paint to dry after each stage. Draw in the arm. Cut out the baby's swaddling clothes, using calico or hessian; glue into place. For Mary's headdress, cut an oblong of cream muslin or calico and fold over one of the short edges twice. Drape the folded edge around her head and glue it on. Use a gold-paper circle for the halo.

JOSEPH Paint his face and brown robe. Short pieces of wool or fine string make the hair, beard and belt. Cut a wooden skewer or thin garden stake for his staff, attaching it with sticky tape. Make his halo as for Mary.

SHEPHERDS They are made in the same way as Joseph, varying the materials (without the halo).

SHEEP Draw in the legs and paint them black. Then cut around each leg and fold the whole flap back (see picture). If this is too fiddly, it might be easier to paint the legs in. Draw in the faces with a black felt-tip pen. Use white tissue paper for the fleece.

THREE WISE MEN Paint the three different figures as shown in the picture. Dress them up with metallic fabrics, printed paper, gold braid, ribbons etc. You could decorate the cloak of the green Wise Man with pieces of torn paper, and the crown with sequins and gold cord. For the purple cloak, try small shapes cut out of coloured paper or you can use precut gummed paper shapes. Gold paint, glitter, sequins and feathers decorate the hats and gifts.

ANGELS These were made from white card (without support flaps), and halos were added as before. Decorate the wings with small petal shapes of white tissue paper. When gluing these on to the wings, overlap slightly to fill them out. You can add a feathery fringe by snipping one side of the tissue petal before you glue them to the body. Attach a long wooden skewer, and lean the angels against the stable.

STABLE Cut a stable silhouette out of stiff card. Make the roof with raffia or straw.

STAR Make a star from stiff card and paint it gold. Glue it to the stable or attach it with a wooden skewer.

Safety Note

The crib should be kept away from young children who could harm themselves if they dislodge the wooden skewers.

GIFT WRAPPING

There is nothing quite like a pile of beautifully wrapped presents under the Christmas tree to evoke a feeling of anticipation and excitement. And somehow, receiving a gift which someone has obviously spent time wrapping up imaginatively is especially pleasurable. Even the most inexpensive Christmas gift becomes an intriguing treat if presented prettily.

Of course there are literally hundreds of different wrapping papers, ribbons, gift cards and trims to choose from. But as you will see here, there are many alternatives to shop-bought paper and ribbon which are just as attractive, far cheaper and more fun to try.

Before embarking on your present wrapping, think about who each gift is for, and then decide on an appropriate treatment. Then consider the size and shape of the item to wrap: will you have enough paper, ribbon, trim, sticky tape and so on? Consider too what sort of effect you would like to create with your pile of presents under the tree: a jolly jumble, or sophisticated tower of packages in carefully co-ordinated papers and trims? Gift-wrapped presents make a wonderful festive decoration in their own right, so it is worth thinking through a colour scheme or other theme.

SOME EASY WRAPPING IDEAS

Use pretty wallpapers as wrapping paper, and cut out matching gift tags.

Plain brown paper looks chic tied up with classy ribbon, or sprinkled with glitter. Apply a very light coating of clear glue to the desired areas, then shake on your glitter. Shake off the excess when dry.

Spatter plain shelving paper or lining paper with paint, or use stencil shapes such as stars, hearts or holly leaves and a spray-on paint.

Sheets of vivid tissue paper, tied up with a silky ribbon, look sophisticated, but be sure to use lots of sheets to give enough weight to the parcel.

If you are tying up a box with ribbon, try putting the ribbon around the corners of the box rather than in the usual criss-cross style. You could also tie the bow off centre, and attach a tiny spray of dried flowers or herbs: bay leaves sprayed gold or silver look smart.

These hatboxes have been covered in wallpaper, and lined with a contrasting paper. Add a large bow, or sprig of dried flowers, and you have the perfect gift box.

COVERED HATBOX

A tower of prettily papered and beribboned hatboxes look wonderful under the tree, or try heaping them around a fireplace, or on top of a table. Using the method here you can cover any size of box, large or small. They make excellent holders to awkward shaped gifts that are tricky to wrap neatly.

YOU WILL NEED: Hatbox, pretty paper (wallpaper, as long as it is not too stiff and does not have a heavy relief pattern, is ideal), wallpaper paste made up according to instructions, brush for applying paste, scissors, pencil, wide ribbon, ruler.

2 Paste the reverse side of the paper and roll the box along the strip, placing it centrally. Snip the overlapping edges into flaps at 2cm (¾ inch) intervals, then stick them down inside the top edge of the box and underneath the base. Cover the vertical sides of the lid in the same way.

1 Cut a strip of paper to cover the outside of the box, allowing an overlap of 2cm (¾ inch) where the edges meet, and 3.5cm (1¼ inches) at the top and bottom edges.

3 Draw around the base of the box on the paper and cut out two rounds. Stick one on to the top of the lid. Trim 0.5cm (¼ inch) off the circumference of the second round, then paste to the base of the box. Using a different paper for the lining if you wish, cut a round for the inside base with a 2cm (¾ inch) overlap all round. Snip this at 2cm (¾ inch) intervals as before and stick in place up the inner sides of the box. Cut paper for the inside, 1cm (½ inch) shorter at the top, with a 2cm (¾ inch) overlap where the edges meet. Stick in place. Line the lid. Finally glue two lengths of ribbon inside it and tie on top.

TIP

If you start early, then you can collect enough sturdy boxes, tins, cartons and pots to cover and use as gift boxes. You don't just have to stick to papering them either – spray paints, glitter, stencils, lacquer paints, ribbon and fabrics can all be used to create something attractive and unusual.

GREEN WRAPPING

At a time of conspicuous consumption it may seem rather futile to try and keep a check on waste paper, while recycling wrapping paper sounds Scrooge-like rather than environmentally friendly. But those of you with Green leanings will be delighted with the following wrapping suggestions that make use, as far as is possible, of environment-friendly materials; many of which are suitable for recycling for next year's presents.

GREEN IDEAS

Try mixing recycled plain paper with brown Manila paper and fabrics such as hessian, or unbleached calico and muslin. Experiment too with paper made in deliciously unlikely materials such as banana, rush, bracken, wool and cotton (available from specialist shops).

When you have wrapped your present, try decorating it with ribbons and bows made from unbleached raffia, soft rope or strips of roughly cut muslin. Brightly coloured cords in cotton, silk or wool provide a vibrant splash.

Home-made trimmings are quick and easy to make and look charming. Bouquets of dried flowers, holly, ivy, pine cones and leaves make unusual trimmings. Wire them into tiny bunches and attach. For the personal touch, pour a drop of coloured sealing wax, or beeswax, on to the parcel and mark with the initial of the receiver.

FLUFFY MUSLIN ROSES Fold wide strips of muslin in half and roll up loosely from one end. Tie the unfolded edge with raffia pulled tight, then attach to the parcel.

SALVAGING PAPER Throwing out expensive wrapping paper is unnecessary if it is in good condition and hasn't been ravaged with sticky tape. If a good size area of paper is intact, cut it out, iron on the wrong side with a warm, not hot, iron, then wrap around a cardboard tube. Trimmings like these are particularly useful for wrapping smaller presents, saving you from cutting into a fresh sheet.

This photograph shows how to use your Green Wrapping simply but with success.

Christmas Cakes, Puddings & Mincemeat

THERE IS NOTHING TO beat the taste of a well-matured Christmas cake or pudding: dark, moist and fragrant with fruit and alcohol, they are the season's most satisfying treats. By starting your cake in good time, say at the end of October or early November, you allow it plenty of time to mature and soak up lots of flavour-enhancing brandy. The same is true of mincemeat, which tastes all the better for a long maturation.

But if Christmas has crept up on you unawares, and you find yourself without cake, pudding or mincemeat a week before the big day, don't despair. There are lots of short cuts you can take – and the results will still taste good.

Christmas Pudding in all its flaming glory.

DECORATING YOUR CAKE

Traditional iced cakes are decorated in several stages. About a week before you plan to eat your cake, you need to cover it with almond paste. One or two days later, you can add the flat white icing - sugarpaste or royal icing (ready-to-roll icing from a supermarket is ideal for this) which forms the background for the rest of your decorations. When this icing has dried after 24 hours, add your chosen trimmings. Leave a further 24 hours, then wrap the whole cake loosely in foil and store in a cool place until needed.

Although the cake featured here is sugarpasted, many Christmas cakes are iced with royal icing (see page 70).

With glazed fruit and nut toppings, you can apply these several weeks in advance, keeping the decorated cakes in an airtight container afterwards to stop all the lovely aroma from disappearing.

THE ULTIMATE CHRISTMAS CAKE

So called because the flavour and appearance of this cake are difficult to beat. The cake is made in several stages, so do read right through the instructions before starting, so you know exactly when to do what.

Rich fruit cakes such as this are not meant to be light but nevertheless they can be made tough if they are beaten once the flour and fruit are added. To avoid this, always beat the butter and sugar together until really soft before adding the eggs, and then fold in the remaining ingredients. Continue folding in gently: do not beat the mixture or the final result will be very heavy.

You can make this cake up to three months in advance: alternatively, you could mature it for three months, then freeze it, thawing the cake overnight in a cool room before decorating it.

A note about the rose decorations: they are tricky and do require specialist tools.

If this sounds too daunting, there is a

TIP

Pre-Christmas stocks of almond paste and icing sugar in shops can quickly run out so buy these early, and purchase a little more than you think you need, in case of accidents.

simpler but still very pretty variation of a holly garland that runs around the top of the cake.

175g (6oz) glacé cherries
175g (6oz) seeded raisins (lexia)
75g (3oz) seedless raisins
75g (3oz) currants
150g (5oz) sultanas
50g (2oz) chopped mixed peel
100ml (4fl oz) brandy
125g (4oz) Brazil nuts
butter or white vegetable fat for greasing
225g (8oz) softened butter
grated rind of 1 lemon
225g (8oz) soft light muscovado sugar
4 eggs (size 3)
30ml (2tbsp) black treacle
225g (8oz) plain white flour
5ml (1tsp) ground mixed spice
50g (2oz) ground almonds

1 Rinse the cherries under cold water to remove all syrup. Drain well, then dry completely with absorbent kitchen paper: quarter each cherry. Roughly chop the seeded raisins. Place the cherries, seeded and seedless raisins, the currants, sultanas and peel in a bowl; mix well. Spoon over 75ml (5tbsp) of the brandy, cover and leave to soak for 3-4 hours. Roughly chop the Brazil nuts; cover.
2 Meanwhile, prepare the tin. Cut two rounds of greaseproof paper to fit the base of a 20cm (8 inch) base-measurement, deep, round cake tin. Measure the circumference of the tin, then cut out a sheet of greaseproof paper big enough to go right around the tin and three times its height. Fold the paper in half and turn up a 2.5cm (1 inch) rim along the folded edge. Snip into this rim at 2.5cm (1 inch) intervals. Brush the tin with melted butter and line the base with one of the rounds of paper; grease. Then line the sides of the tin with the strip of paper, the snipped edge resting flat on the base circle. Grease the snipped edge and place the remaining paper on top of it. This final sheet does not need greasing.
3 Beat the butter with the grated lemon rind in a bowl until very soft and pale in colour. Gradually beat in the sugar until well

blended. In a separate bowl, whisk the eggs, then slowly beat them into the creamed ingredients. Add the treacle, beating again until evenly blended.

4 Sift the flour and spice together and stir half into the creamed ingredients with the chopped Brazil nuts and the ground almonds. Gently fold in all of the fruit, followed by the remaining flour. Spoon into the prepared cake tin and then level the surface. Tie a band of brown paper around the outside of the tin.

5 Bake at 150°C (300°F) mark 2 for 3-3½ hours or until a fine skewer inserted into the centre comes out clean. If necessary, lay a sheet of brown paper over the cake tin after about 2 hours cooking to prevent over-browning.

6 Leave the cake in the tin to cool completely, then pierce the surface with a fine skewer and spoon over the remaining brandy. Leave for about 1 hour to allow the brandy to soak in, then turn out the cake. Remove the lining paper and wrap tightly in fresh greaseproof paper and foil. Leave in a cool, dry place for at least a week (it can be left up to three months) before adding the icing. Feed with brandy a few times, as above, for extra flavour.

SERVES 12-16

Dark and fruity, The Ultimate Christmas Cake tastes as good as it looks. The decorations shown here are quite tricky to make, but as an alternative, try making a simple garland of holly leaves (see page 72).

DECORATING THE CAKE

The cake can be decorated about a week before Christmas. For the bow, you will need about 1½ metres (5 foot) of red ribbon, 6.5-7.5cm (2½-3 inches) wide.

30ml (2tbsp) apricot jam
icing sugar
225g (8oz) white almond paste (see Note)
cornflour
450g (1lb) ready-to-roll icing (see Note)
1 quantity royal icing (see Note)
7 Christmas roses (see recipe)
about 12 holly leaves and 15 holly berries (see page 72)

1 If the cake has an uneven top, cut it level, then turn it over so the flat base becomes the top. Place on a 25.5cm (10 inch) cake board ready for decorating.

2 Sieve the apricot jam into a small saucepan and add 10ml (2tsp) water. Heat gently, stirring, until the jam begins to melt. Boil for 1 minute. Brush the top of the cake with the hot apricot jam.

3 Sift a little icing sugar on to a clean work surface. Roll out the almond paste to a round slightly larger than the top of the cake. Using the cake tin as a guide, cut the almond paste to fit.

4 Lift the almond paste on to the cake and smooth it over with a rolling pin: neaten the edges with a small palette knife. Leave to dry, uncovered, at cool room temperature for about two days.

5 Sprinkle a clean work surface with cornflour, roll out the ready-to-roll icing to a round slightly larger than the top of the cake. Cut to fit and place on top of the almond paste. Smooth and neaten the edges as before. To store for a day or two, pin a strip of foil around the exposed cake edges. Cover the top loosely with greaseproof paper.

6 Make the royal icing and cover with cling film until required. Use about 30ml (2tbsp) for the roses. The remainder will keep, covered, for two weeks in the refrigerator; stir before using. It can be used to pipe a shell border around the cake, or to attach extra holly leaves to the board. Or use to cover the cake board: soften with a little water to a dropping consistency, spoon on to the board and smooth up to the cake base.

7 Using a little of the royal icing, attach the Christmas roses, holly leaves and berries to the top of the cake. Leave to dry at cool room temperature for 24 hours. Store wrapped as in step 5, for up to a week.

8 To complete, tie the ribbon around the cake and finish with a large bow.

VARIATION
HOLLY GARLAND For a simple, effective decoration which is quick to prepare, double the number of holly leaves and berries. Form the leaves and berries into a garland around the top of the cake, using royal icing to secure.

Note

White almond paste is available from most major supermarkets. It has a more home-made look than the yellow variety, which can look a little garish.

Ready-to-roll icing or *ready-to-use icing* is a ready made sugarpaste or moulding icing. It is available from most major supermarkets and from specialist cake decorating shops or by mail order from BR Mathews, Mary Ford Cake Artistry Centre and Squires Kitchen (*see Useful Addresses* on page 73).

The royal icing used for the Christmas roses and in the sugarpasted cake featured here requires only 1 egg white and 225g (8oz) icing sugar, omitting the lemon juice and glycerine.

ROYAL ICING

This quantity is sufficient to cover a 23cm (9 inch) round or 20cm (8 inch) square cake.

4 egg whites
900g (2lb) icing sugar
15ml (1tbsp) lemon juice
10ml (2tsp) glycerine

1 Whisk the egg whites in a bowl until slightly frothy. Then sift and stir in about a quarter of the icing sugar with a wooden spoon. Continue adding more sugar gradually, beating well after each addition, until about three-quarters of the sugar has been added.

2 Beat in the lemon juice and continue beating for about 10 minutes until the icing is smooth.

3 Beat in the remaining sugar until the required consistency is achieved, depending on how the icing will be used.

4 Finally, stir in the glycerine to prevent the icing hardening. Cover and keep for 24 hours to allow air bubbles to rise to the surface.

MAKES ABOUT 900 G (2LB)

CHRISTMAS ROSES

The same ready-to-roll icing used for decorating the cake and making the holly leaves can be used here in place of the petal paste. However, you will find that the end result will not be as fine or delicate and the flowers will be a little softer. This recipe uses seven roses on the cake, but it is best to make about ten in order to allow for possible breakages.

There are several items of equipment you will need to make the roses: small rolling pin and board (preferably nonstick, plastic or stainless steel), medium rose-petal cutter, cocktail sticks, sponge block, ball modelling tool (optional), fine paintbrushes and a small palette knife.

cornflour or icing sugar
about 75g (3oz) petal paste (see Note)
lemon-yellow dusting powder
reserved royal icing (see step 6 of *Decorating the Cake*)
about 35 double-headed yellow stamens

1 Lightly dust a work surface or small board with cornflour or icing sugar. Roll out a small piece of petal paste very thinly. Keep the rest of the paste tightly covered with cling film.

2 Dust a petal cutter with icing sugar and cut out five petals.

3 Gently roll a cocktail stick over the round edge of the petal to make a thinner, slightly frilled edge.

4 Place each petal on a sponge block and gently curl each petal to give a shallow cup shape, using your fingertips or a ball modelling tool. Then cover each petal loosely with some cling film to prevent it from drying out.

5 Brush one side of the first petal with water, then put the next petal in position, overlapping the edges. Repeat, adding two more petals. Cup the half-assembled flower, first dusting your fingers with cornflour or icing sugar. Put the last petal in position so that it overlaps the fourth petal and tucks under the first to form the rose. Continue with the remaining petal paste to make about nine more roses. (The flowers must be made one at a time and the petal paste kept covered as it dries very quickly.) Leave to dry for about 1 hour.

6 Using a dry brush, carefully dust the inside of the flowers with the lemon-yellow dusting powder. Brush from the centre outwards to obtain a graduated effect.

7 Using the end of a teaspoon, place a small blob of the reserved royal icing in the centre of each flower. Cut four to five stamens in half to give eight to ten heads, trim to size and then position them carefully in the icing. Leave to dry for approximately 2 hours. Repeat the process until you have completed all ten roses. The roses can be stored for up to three months.

Decorating extras such as holly leaf cutters, rose-petal cutters, sponge blocks, ball modelling tools, lemon-yellow dusting powder, double-headed stamens, albumen powder, gum arabic, confectioner's glaze and food colourings are available from specialist cake decorating shops or by mail order from BR Mathews, Mary Ford Cake Artistry Centre and Squires Kitchen (see *Useful Addresses* on page 73).

Note

Petal paste is a finer form of ready-to-roll or ready-to-use icing which dries to a harder finish. It is available from specialist cake decorating shops and by mail order from Woodnutt's (see *Useful Addresses* on page 73).

HOLLY LEAVES AND BERRIES

These leaves are made using a holly-leaf cutter. Make the leaves look even more festive by giving them a sheen. Glaze them with either gum arabic or confectioner's glaze (see Decorating extras on page 71).

about 75g (3oz) ready-to-roll icing (see *Decorating the Cake* Note)

green mint and Christmas red food colouring paste

icing sugar

gum arabic or confectioner's glaze (optional)

1 Reserve a small quantity of icing for berries. Dip a cocktail stick into the green paste and add a little to the remaining icing. Blend in the colour by kneading and mixing the sugarpaste between fingers and thumbs. Repeat, adding a little more colour until a good shade is obtained. To avoid getting green fingers, first place the icing and colour together inside a polythene bag and knead. Repeat with red paste and reserved icing.

2 Lightly dust a work surface or board with icing sugar. Roll out the coloured icing thinly and cut out about twelve holly leaves, using a holly-leaf cutter. Mark the central and small veins lightly into the sugarpaste with a cocktail stick. Twist the leaves a little from the centre and leave to dry for 24 hours over the handle of a wooden spoon to create a natural, curved shape. Roll about fifteen berries from red icing. Store in an airtight container for up to three months.

3 If you glaze the holly leaves, do this as you decorate the cake. The glaze tends to crack if left for longer than a week. Either brush with confectioner's glaze according to manufacturer's instructions, or mix one part gum arabic with three parts water in a small bowl and dissolve slowly over hot water. Strain and cool the glaze before using. Place the leaves to dry on nonstick baking parchment for about 1 hour.

Useful Addresses

BR Mathews, 12 Gypsy Hill, London SE19 1NN (081-670-0788).

Mary Ford Cake Artistry Centre, 28/30 Southbourne Grove, Bournemouth BH6 3RA (0202-417766).

Squires Kitchen, Squires House, 3 Waverley Lane, Farnham, Surrey GU9 8BB (0252-711749).

Woodnutt's, 97 Church Road, Hove, Sussex BN3 2BA (0273-205353/4).

Or check in *Yellow Pages* for local firms in your area that specialise in cake-decorating equipment.

Teatime treats – the glazed cherry and pineapple topping on the fruit cake makes a delicious alternative to icing and marzipan.

than suet for extra flavour, and three different kinds of nut for interesting taste and texture. Chop them as coarsely as you like.

When first mixed, the pudding will seem very moist, but overnight the fruit absorbs a lot of the liquid, giving a drier texture.

You can either make one large pudding, as shown here, or divide the mixture into ten individual ones, which would make perfect presents. If you make the small version, you will need a double piece of muslin about 25.5cm (10 inches) square for each, and to steam them for about six hours. Reheat on Christmas Day, or whenever they are needed, for four hours.

As an alternative cooking method for the large pudding, steam the mixture in a 1.4-1.6 litre (2½-2¾ pint) pudding basin. To do this, first grease then line the base of the bowl with greaseproof paper. Spoon in the mixture, cover with a layer of pleated greaseproof paper and foil, tying the foil securely under the rim of the bowl. Steam for about eight hours. Once cold, cover with fresh foil and store. When required, steam for about five hours.

THE ULTIMATE CHRISTMAS PUDDING

For the pudding	
50g (2oz) almonds	
50g (2oz) pecans	
50g (2oz) Brazil nuts	
75g (3oz) carrot	
75g (3oz) stoned no-soak prunes	
350g (12oz) seedless raisins, currants and sultanas, mixed	
25g (1oz) chopped mixed peel	
125g (4oz) butter	
finely grated rind of 1 lemon	
125g (4oz) soft dark brown sugar	
2 eggs, beaten	
50g (2oz) fresh brown breadcrumbs	
125g (4oz) plain wholemeal flour	
50g (2oz) plain white flour	
15ml (1tbsp) ground mixed spice	
200ml (7 fl oz) Guinness	
30ml (2tbsp) brandy	
30ml (2tbsp) black treacle	
about 10 coins to serve (optional)	
holly to decorate and brandy to flame	
For the brandy butter	
125g (4oz) unsalted butter	
125g (4oz) icing sugar	
25g (1oz) ground almonds	
60ml (4tbsp) double cream	
45ml (3tbsp) brandy	

1 *If the almonds have skins, cover with boiling water and leave to stand for 5-10 minutes. Drain off water and pop the nuts out of their skins. If the skins stick, blanch the nuts a little longer. Dry on kitchen paper, then roughly chop with the pecan and Brazil nuts. Peel and coarsely grate the carrot. Snip the prunes into small pieces. Place these ingredients in a large bowl with the raisins, currants, sultanas and mixed peel.*

TO FREEZE:
Pack and freeze the brandy butter. Wrap and freeze the pudding after maturing for one month.

TO USE:
Thaw the brandy butter overnight in the refrigerator. Thaw the pudding overnight at cool room temperature, reheat as opposite.
SERVES 10

2 *In another bowl, beat the butter and finely grated lemon rind until soft. Gradually beat in the sugar, keeping the mixture light and fluffy. (If the sugar is lumpy, sieve before use.) Add the eggs gradually. Spoon this mixture into the bowl of fruit and nuts. Add all the remaining ingredients, beating well until thoroughly mixed. Cover and leave in a cool place overnight (not the refrigerator).*

3 *Scald, rinse and dry the coins (5p or 20p pieces). Wrap each one in a small square of greaseproof paper to enclose completely. Fold the ends of the paper under the coin and tuck in securely to prevent the coins from bursting out. Alternatively, scrub the scalded coins well and push into each portion just before it is served.*

5 *Take a large pan – a preserving pan is ideal – and lay a wooden spoon or piece of wood across the top. Tie on the pudding so that it is suspended in the pan. Pour in boiling water – ideally the pudding should not touch the water, but do not worry if about 1cm (½ inch) is submerged. Cover the pan with foil. Steam the pudding for about 8 hours, topping up with boiling water to prevent the pan from boiling dry.*

7 *To make the brandy butter, beat the butter until really soft, then gradually beat in the sugar and ground almonds. Gently work in the cream, half at a time. Finally, beat in the brandy, 15ml (1tbsp) at a time – if the mixture shows signs of curdling, beat really vigorously. Cover the brandy butter and refrigerate for up to two weeks. Remove from the refrigerator at least 30 minutes before serving.*

8 *On the day, steam the pudding for about 5 hours. Mould again into a neat shape. Unwrap and place on a heatproof plate. Wrap foil around the stem of a piece of holly and push into the pudding. Warm about 60ml (4tbsp) brandy in a saucepan. Pour over the pudding, then light with a match. Baste with the flamed brandy and serve with brandy butter.*

4 *The following day, beat the pudding mixture well, then carefully stir in the covered coins. Take a large piece of fine muslin – about 51 × 102cm (20 ×40 inches), fold into a 51cm (20 inch) square and dust liberally with flour. Spoon the mixture into the centre. Bring the edges of the muslin up to the top of the pudding, moulding it into a round. Tie the top securely with string, leaving a long piece free.*

6 *Drain the water from the pan and leave the pudding suspended to cool slightly – about 30 minutes. While still warm, mould it into a neat round, then leave suspended until quite cold. Remove the wet muslin and carefully retie the pudding in clean, dry, well-floured muslin and overwrap with foil. Store in the refrigerator for up to one month.*

LIGHT CHRISTMAS PUDDING

This is a less heavily fruited version of The Ultimate Christmas Pudding and tastes quite delicious served either with Brandy Butter (see page 86) or Sherry Nutmeg Sauce, see right. It should have its initial steaming no more than a week before it is to be eaten.

75g (3oz) currants
75g (3oz) seedless raisins
175g (6oz) sultanas
finely grated rind and juice of 1 large orange
60ml (4tbsp) brandy
45ml (3tbsp) black treacle
175g (6oz) margarine
75g (3oz) soft dark brown sugar
3 eggs
175g (6oz) plain wholemeal flour
75g (3oz) fresh brown breadcrumbs
10ml (2tsp) baking powder
75g (3oz) chopped hazelnuts
10ml (2tsp) ground mixed spice
Brandy Butter or Sherry Nutmeg Sauce to serve

1 Place the dried fruits, orange rind, 90ml (6tbsp) orange juice, the brandy and black treacle in a large bowl; stir well to mix. Cover and marinate overnight.

2 Grease and base line a 1.7 litre (3 pint) pudding basin. Beat the margarine and sugar in a bowl until well mixed. Gradually beat in the eggs – the mixture may look curdled. Stir into the fruit with the remaining ingredients until evenly mixed.

3 Spoon into the prepared pudding basin. Cover with pleated, greased greaseproof paper and foil. Tie securely.

4 Boil the pudding for about 2½ hours or steam for about 3 hours, until firm to the touch. Cool. When cold, replace the foil (not the greaseproof paper) and store in the refrigerator for up to one week.

5 On the day, boil or steam for about 2 hours. Turn out and serve with Brandy Butter or Sherry Nutmeg Sauce.

TO FREEZE:
Pack and freeze.

TO USE:
Thaw overnight at cool room temperature, then reheat as above.
SERVES ABOUT 8

SHERRY NUTMEG SAUCE

40g (1½oz) butter or margarine
40g (1½oz) plain white flour
568ml (1 pint) milk
150ml (¼ pint) single cream
40g (1½oz) caster sugar
60ml (4tbsp) sherry
grated nutmeg

1 Melt the butter in a pan, stir in the flour and cook for 2 minutes, stirring. Gradually add the milk and simmer for 2 minutes, stirring all the time. Stir in the cream.

2 Remove from the heat and stir in the sugar and sherry with nutmeg to taste.

3 Serve with Christmas pudding or mince pies.

TO FREEZE:
Cool, pack and freeze at the end of step 2.

TO USE:
Thaw overnight at cool room temperature. Reheat without boiling, whisking until smooth.
SERVES 8

FROZEN CHRISTMAS
PUDDING

Quick to make and delicious to eat, this iced Christmas pudding is a lighter alternative to the traditional steamed version. The apricots add extra succulence, and the rum-soaked ingredients contrast perfectly with the creamy coldness of the ice cream.

50g (2oz) no-soak dried apricots
175g (6oz) mixed currants, seedless raisins and sultanas
finely grated rind of 1 orange
finely grated rind of 1 lemon
60ml (4tbsp) rum or brandy
5ml (1tsp) ground mixed spice
300ml (½ pint) double cream
500g (1lb 2oz) carton or can ready-to-serve custard
75g (3oz) caster sugar
brandy to accompany (optional)

1 Snip the apricots into small pieces. In a large bowl, mix with the remaining dried fruit. Add the orange and lemon rind, the rum and mixed spice. Cover and leave to soak for about 15 minutes – longer if possible to give the flavours time to develop.

2 Whisk the cream until it just holds its shape and fold into the fruit with the custard and sugar.

3 Pour the mixture into an airtight freezerproof container, cover and freeze for about 2 hours. Stir gently to distribute the fruits and break down any ice crystals. Recover, then freeze until firm, about 6 hours.

4 To serve, remove from the freezer and leave at room temperature for about 15 minutes. Serve in scoops with a little extra brandy or rum poured over if wished.

SERVES 8

Cool and sophisticated, this Frozen Christmas Pudding makes a refreshing alternative to the traditional steamed version. A dash of brandy or rum poured over provides a contrast of flavours.

CHRISTMAS FRUIT COMPOTE

A very superior kind of fruit salad, the wonderful fresh flavours of pineapple, green grapes and rambutans or lychees will quickly restore jaded palates. For those who crave a little richness, the compote is complemented perfectly with double cream sweetened with a little caster sugar and then ground cinnamon whisked in. For the final festive touch, add a few fresh cranberries for colour.

300g (11oz) can rambutans or lychees in fruit juice
1 pineapple
50g (2oz) caster sugar
15ml (1tbsp) brandy
5cm (2 inch) piece cinnamon stick
pinch ground ginger
225g (8oz) seedless green grapes
a few fresh cranberries (optional)
sweet cinnamon cream to serve

1 Strain the rambutans or lychees, reserving the juice. Cut fruit in half. Peel, core and roughly chop the pineapple.
2 Place the reserved juice in a large saucepan with the sugar, brandy and spices. Heat gently until all the sugar has dissolved, then bring to the boil.
3 Add all the fruit to the saucepan. Bring back to the boil, simmer gently for 1-2 minutes.
4 Serve warm or chilled, accompanied by sweet cinnamon cream.

NOT SUITABLE FOR FREEZING
SERVES 8

THREE ULTIMATE PUDDINGS

Sometimes, especially at this time of year, you want a pudding that will really impress. Here are three very different ones that are guaranteed to look and taste marvellous. One of them – the Port-Wine Jelly – even has the added attraction of not being too fattening. Enjoy!

CHOCOLATE MILLE-FEUILLE

This is an intriguing combination of flavours and colours: tangy orange sauce, bittersweet dark chocolate and a melting creamy filling of white chocolate. Devised by one of Britain's top chefs, Gary Holihead, it's a real dinner party winner. Simple to assemble, it can be made the day before serving and stored (separately from the sauce) in the refrigerator, or well in advance and frozen. Do not let it stand at room temperature once thawed as it will quickly soften and lose its shape. When melting chocolate, the rule is to do it slowly over a very gentle heat without stirring; when it has completely melted, stir slowly for about 1 minute until it is smooth and creamy. Be careful – if the water is hotter than a gentle simmer or the chocolate is overbeaten, it will become granular and unmanageable.

175g (6oz) plain chocolate
125g (4oz) white chocolate
300ml (½ pint) double cream
cocoa powder, to dust
6 oranges, preferably blood variety
10ml (2tsp) cornflour
25g (1oz) caster sugar

1 Break up the plain chocolate roughly. Place in a small bowl and melt slowly over a saucepan of gently simmering water. When completely melted, stir for about 1 minute until the chocolate becomes smoooth and creamy.
2 Mark out four 15 × 10cm (6 × 4 inch) rectangles on a sheet of foil or nonstick baking parchment. Place on a large flat baking sheet. With a small palette knife or round-bladed knife, spread the melted chocolate thinly and evenly into the rectangles. Refrigerate for about 1 hour.
3 Break up the white chocolate roughly and melt as before. Leave to cool slightly.
4 Whip the double cream until it begins to hold its shape. Stir about 30ml (2tbsp) into the white chocolate to loosen. Fold in the remaining cream, stirring gently until well mixed and smooth.

5 To assemble, carefully peel away the foil or baking parchment from the set chocolate leaves. Place one of the leaves upon foil or baking parchment set on a chilled, flat baking sheet. Spread over one third of the white-chocolate cream. Continue layering the leaves with the cream, ending with a chocolate leaf. Press down lightly. Dust heavily with sifted cocoa powder and refrigerate to set for at least 2 hours or preferably overnight.

6 With a swivel potato peeler, peel and set aside the rind from one orange. Squeeze the juice from the orange and the five others into a measuring jug and make up to 300ml (½ pint) with water if necessary. Strain the juice into a small saucepan. Blend the cornflour to a smooth paste with 30ml (2tbsp) water. Stir into the orange juice with the sugar.

7 Bring slowly to the boil, stirring continuously. Simmer until slightly thickened and clear. Pour the orange sauce into a bowl, cover loosely and set aside to cool.

8 Cut the reserved orange rind into needle-thin shreds. Drop into a saucepan of boiling water, then simmer for 3-4 minutes until tender. Drain and cool under cold water, add to the sauce.

9 To serve, dust the mille-feuille with more cocoa powder. Heat a serrated knife in boiling water for 4-5 seconds. Dry, then use to cut the mille-feuille into four 5 × 7.5 cm (2 × 3 inch) rectangles. Pour a little of the orange sauce on to four flat plates and place a portion of the mille feuille on top. Serve immediately, accompanied by the remaining sauce, or refrigerate for a maximum of 1 hour.

A melting mixture of dark chocolate, layered with rich white chocolate cream on a pool of tangy orange sauce, makes this Chocolate Mille-feuille a dessert in a thousand.

TO FREEZE:
At the end of step 5, freeze the mille-feuille uncovered until firm, then remove from the freezer, wrap and return. Freeze the orange sauce at the end of step 8.

TO USE:
Thaw the orange sauce at cool room temperature. Chill before serving. Allow the mille-feuille to stand for 30 minutes at room temperature until soft enough to cut. Continue as in step 9.
SERVES 4

PORT-WINE JELLY

A truly spectacular dessert this one. A trembling, dark red and jewel-bright castle of rich jelly, wreathed with pears and grapes, and tasting deliciously of port.

For best results use a generous quantity of port with a good quality red wine. You will also need small, ripe dessert pears, as these are easier to slice neatly for the wreath effect, and tiny seedless black grapes. If these are unavailable, buy the smallest you can and halve or quarter. When measuring the gelatine, be precise – too much and you will get an unpleasant, firm texture, too little and the jelly will not set firm enough to keep its shape. Allow about six hours to set, or leave overnight, then dip the mould

quickly into warm water and turn out. For the faint-hearted the jelly can be served in individual glasses, but use only 35ml (7tsp) gelatine for a softer texture and set a little fruit in the base of each glass first.

A rich, ruby-red port-wine jelly. The secret of a perfect set is to use exactly the right amount of gelatine and not to lose your nerve when turning the jelly on to the dish.

600ml (1 pint) medium red wine, such as Côtes du Rhône
450ml (¾ pint) ruby port
175g (6oz) caster or granulated sugar
45ml (3tbsp) brandy
juice of 2 large lemons
900g (2lb) small ripe dessert pears
1 cinnamon stick
175g (6oz) small black grapes
37.5ml (7½tsp) powdered gelatine
single cream to serve

1 Place the wine and port in a large saucepan with 300ml (½ pint) water and the sugar. Add the brandy with 90ml (6tbsp) strained lemon juice, then warm gently until the sugar dissolves. Stir the ingredients occasionally with a wooden spoon to ease the sugar off the base of the pan. Once the sugar has completely dissolved, bring the liquid to the boil and bubble for 1 minute. Remove from the heat.

2 Peel and quarter the pears. Cut into short, thin slices – about 2.5-4cm (1-1½ inches) long. Add all the pears to the wine syrup with the cinnamon stick. Bring to the boil, cover and poach gently until the pears are quite tender – about 10 minutes.

3 Meanwhile, halve the grapes, if you are unable to find the very small variety, cover and keep on one side. Using a draining spoon, lift all the pear slices out of the

syrup. Place the slices in a serving bowl.

4 Line a large nylon sieve with a double layer of fine muslin and place it over a large bowl. Slowly pour the wine syrup through the muslin. Allow it to drip slowly through at its own pace – don't push the juices through with a spoon as this will cloud the liquid.

5 Meanwhile, pour 150ml (¼ pint) water into a small basin and sprinkle over the gelatine, taking particular care to measure it precisely. Leave it to soak for about 10 minutes or until sponge-like in texture. Stand the basin in a pan of gently simmering water until the gelatine clears and liquefies. Stir into 1.1 litres (2 pints) of the strained wine syrup, mixing thoroughly. Leave to cool. Pour the remaining syrup over the fruit in the serving bowl, cover and set aside to cool in the refrigerator.

6 Rinse a 1.4 litre (2½ pint) nonstick jelly mould with cold water. Pour in three-quarters of the cool syrup mixture and refrigerate to set – this should take approximately 3 hours. Keep the remaining syrup at room temperature to prevent it from reaching setting point.

7 Arrange some of the pear slices and a few grapes around the edge of the set jelly to form a wreath effect. Place this in the refrigerator, then carefully spoon over the remaining syrup mixture. Reserve the remaining grapes and pears for decoration.

8 Don't move the mould again until this second layer of jelly has set, or the fruits will float around and you will lose the wreath effect. Leave in the refrigerator for at least 6 hours, preferably overnight, so that the jelly has a chance to set sufficiently to turn out.

9 Have ready a medium-sized round serving platter. Moisten the surface lightly with cold water. Quickly dip the moulded jelly into a bowl of warm water, then invert on to the plate. If the jelly refuses to come out of the mould, give it a few firm shakes sideways, or, if necessary, dip into the warm water again: gently shake the serving platter to centralise it.

10 Serve the jelly with the extra grapes and pears, together with single cream.

NOT SUITABLE FOR FREEZING
SERVES 8

Tip

Always moisten the serving plate before tipping a jelly on to it; that way, if it does not land centrally it can be eased into the middle.

TRIFLE

Boozy, fruity and creamy: a proper English trifle like the one here should have lashings of sherry, fruit, cream and proper home-made custard to give it an authentic and totally irresistible flavour. Don't make your trifle in a hurry. The flavours need time to blend and marry together. And do use the very best ingredients – a good medium sherry and decent brandy (if you are using it), and firm fruits, either fresh or frozen, not soggy canned ones. The sponge base can be made of trifle sponges, Madeira cake or Genoese sponge, with the addition of crushed macaroons or ratafias if you like for an additional delicious almond flavour. To release the full flavour of the fruit, it is a good idea to crush it lightly before adding it to the sponge.
The final vital ingredient is the custard. The home-made variety made with eggs, milk, vanilla and sugar has a silken smoothness lacking in the canned or packet kinds, and perfectly complements the berries and sponge. If you are pressed for time and want to use a packet variety, add some cream for extra richness, and remember not to make it too thick. It should set to a gentle firmness not a gelatinous mass.
For decoration, glacé fruits and toasted nuts look best.

Tip

Don't throw the vanilla pod away after use. Rinse, then pat dry. Place in a bag of sugar, reseal and within days you will have vanilla sugar.

1 Split the trifle sponges in two and lay the bottom halves over the base of a deep glass bowl. Warm the jam or jelly until just melted, sieve and carefully pour over the trifle sponges. Top with the remaining sponges. If using Madeira cake, slice thinly before using.

2 Spoon the sherry and brandy evenly over the sponges, making sure they are saturated. Scatter over the fruit, halving some of the berries if wished. Cover and refrigerate for 1 hour or more.

3 Split open the vanilla pod to reveal the seeds. Add to the milk or cream and bring to the boil. Take off the heat: cover and infuse for about 20 minutes.

4 Preferably using an electric beater, mix the eggs and sugar until pale and foaming. Strain on the milk.

5 Stir the custard well and return to the pan. Over a low heat, stir the custard until it begins to thicken – this will take some time (15-20 minutes) as you must not allow the mixture to boil or it will curdle. Once lightly thickened, pour out into a bowl and cool – it will thicken up considerably when chilled.

6 Lightly whisk, then pour the cool custard over the fruit. Cover and chill for several hours, preferably overnight.

7 Whip the cream with a little sifted icing sugar to taste until it just holds its shape. Carefully spread this over the custard and decorate with the fruits and/or nuts.

NOT SUITABLE FOR FREEZING
SERVES 8-10

10 trifle sponges or about 1½ Madeira cakes, 400g (14oz) total weight
225g (8oz) fruit jam or jelly, such as raspberry, strawberry or blackberry
150ml (¼ pint) sherry and brandy, mixed
450g (1lb) fresh or frozen berries, such as raspberries, blackberries, loganberries or tayberries
1 vanilla pod (see Tip)
568ml (1 pint) creamy milk or single cream
8 eggs
175g (6oz) caster sugar
450ml (¾ pint) double cream
a little icing sugar
glacé fruits and/or toasted nuts to decorate

The ultimate trifle – lashings of real, creamy custard, fruit, fresh cream, and sherry. Let the flavours marry together for several hours before serving.

FORCEMEAT BALLS

50g (2oz) butter
175g (6oz) onions, skinned and roughly chopped
50g (2oz) walnut pieces, roughly chopped
2.5ml (½tsp) chilli powder
900g (2lb) pork sausages or sausagemeat
chopped fresh parsley
salt and pepper
flour
oil

1 Heat the butter in a frying pan, add the onions and fry until beginning to brown. Mix in the nuts and chilli powder, stir-fry for 1 minute. Turn out on to a plate. Leave to cool.

2 Place the sausagemeat in a bowl. Stir in the onions with 60ml (4tbsp) parsley. Season well.

3 With floured hands, shape the sausagemeat into thirty-two balls. Place on a baking sheet, cover and chill.

4 Heat a thin film of oil in a large roasting tin. Add the forcemeat balls. Bake at 180°C (350°F) mark 4 for about 45 minutes, turning occasionally. Drain on absorbent kitchen paper. Toss in parsley and serve as an accompaniment to turkey.

TO FREEZE:

Use fresh, not previously frozen sausagemeat. Pack and freeze at end of step 3.

TO USE:

Thaw overnight at cool room temperature. Cook as above.
SERVES 10-12

APRICOT AND CELERY STUFFING

125g (4oz) no-soak dried apricots
125g (4oz) celery
175g (6oz) fresh breadcrumbs
2.5ml (½tsp) dried sage
1.25ml (¼tsp) ground mixed spice
25g (1oz) butter
salt and pepper
1 egg
15ml (1tbsp) Dijon mustard

1 Dice the apricots finely. Slice the celery finely. Mix with the breadcrumbs, sage, spice, butter and seasoning.

2 Lightly beat the egg and mustard together and use to bind the stuffing. If necessary, moisten with a little stock. Cover and chill.

NOT SUITABLE FOR FREEZING
MAKES 450G (1LB)

Glazed Stuffed Turkey with Forcemeat Balls, Fan-tailed Roast Potatoes, Carrots with Lemon and Garlic and Cranberry Sauce.

The following two recipes make a delicious variation on the Apricot and Celery Stuffing. The first, pecan and celery, is cooked in a shallow dish and would make a good alternative to forcemeat balls. The second, chestnut and apricot, makes a lavish quantity for a 4.5kg (10lb) bird. You could cook any surplus in a tray, as for the pecan and celery stuffing.

PECAN AND CELERY STUFFING

If pecan nuts are difficult to obtain, use the slightly more bitter walnuts.

45-60ml (3-4tbsp) oil
3 medium onions, skinned and finely chopped
225g (8oz) ready-to-eat prunes (no-soak)
1 small head celery, chopped
150g (5oz) pecan nuts, roughly chopped
about 275g (10oz) fresh breadcrumbs
45ml (3tbsp) chopped fresh parsley
2 small eggs, size 6, beaten
salt and pepper
butter or margarine

1 Heat the oil in a pan, add the onions and fry until beginning to soften but not brown. Stone and chop the prunes.
2 Mix all the ingredients together and season to taste. If the mixture is too wet, add more breadcrumbs.
3 Press the stuffing lightly into a shallow, greased ovenproof dish and dot with butter. Bake for about 35-40 minutes or until crisp and golden brown on top.

NOT SUITABLE FOR FREEZING
MAKES ABOUT 1.1KG(2½LB)

CHESTNUT AND APRICOT STUFFING

If it is difficult to remove all the membrane from the roasted chestnuts, ease the rest off once they have been cooked.

700g (1½lb) fresh chestnuts
750ml (1¼ pints) vegetable stock
60ml (4tbsp) oil
3 medium onions, skinned and finely chopped
300g (11oz) ready-to-eat apricots (no-soak)
350g (12oz) fresh breadcrumbs
90ml (6tbsp) chopped fresh parsley
2 small eggs, size 6, beaten
salt and pepper
butter or margarine

1 Peel the chestnuts by making a slit in the side of each nut and roasting them in a hot 220°C (425°F) mark 7 oven for about 10-15 minutes or until the skins burst. Remove the skins and membrane. Simmer the chestnuts in the stock until tender, about 20 minutes. Drain and chop into large pieces.
2 Heat the oil in a pan, add the onions and fry until beginning to soften. Cool slightly. Snip the apricots into small pieces. Mix both with the remaining stuffing ingredients. Season to taste, adding more breadcrumbs if the mixture is too wet.
3 Press about one-third of this stuffing into the neck end of the turkey, pushing it under the skin and up over the breast. Truss the turkey.
4 Place the remaining stuffing in a shallow, greased ovenproof dish and dot with butter. Bake for about 35-40 minutes.

NOT SUITABLE FOR FREEZING
MAKES ABOUT 1.4KG (3LB)

FAN-TAILED ROAST POTATOES

about 1.8kg (4lb) old potatoes, peeled
salt and pepper
oil
coarse oatmeal and/or sesame seeds

1 Cut the potatoes into large, even chunks. Cover with cold salted water, bring to the boil and boil for 2 minutes. Drain, place under cold running water to cool slightly.

2 Using a sharp knife, slice down each potato at 0.3-0.5cm (⅛-¼ inch) intervals, cutting three-quarters of the way through.

3 Heat a good film of oil in a large roasting tin. Add the potatoes and turn over in the oil. Sprinkle with oatmeal and/or sesame seeds.

4 Roast at 180°C (350°F) mark 4 for about 2 hours, basting occasionally. If necessary, raise the oven temperature to 220°C (425°F) mark 7 for 15-20 minutes to brown. (Turkey should now be out of the oven, firming up.) Keep warm.

NOT SUITABLE FOR FREEZING
SERVES 10-12

SPROUTS WITH BACON ROLLS AND MUSHROOMS

225g (8oz) streaky bacon
1.4kg (3lb) Brussels sprouts, trimmed and halved
salt and pepper
about 75g (3oz) butter
225g (8oz) button mushrooms, sliced
60ml (4tbsp) plain white flour
30ml (2tbsp) Dijon mustard
30ml (2tbsp) lemon juice
60ml (4tbsp) single cream

1 Halve the bacon rashers and roll up each piece. Thread the rolls on to long metal or wooden skewers.

2 Boil the sprouts in a pan of salted water until just tender. Drain, reserving 600ml (1 pint) cooking liquor. Cover and keep warm.

3 Place the bacon under the grill and cook for 3-4 minutes. Heat 75g (3oz) butter in a medium saucepan and add the mushrooms. Cook over a high heat until all the moisture has evaporated. Remove from the pan using a draining spoon.

4 Stir the flour into the pan, adding a little more butter if necessary. Cook for 1 minute. Blend in the vegetable water, mustard and seasoning. Bring to the boil, stirring all the time. Replace the mushrooms, add the bacon rolls and warm through. Remove from the heat, mix in the lemon juice and cream. Adjust the seasoning.

5 Pour over the sprouts. Cover and keep warm until required.

NOT SUITABLE FOR FREEZING
SERVES 10-12

CARROTS WITH LEMON AND GARLIC

Just cover the carrots with water so it evaporates before they become overcooked.

1.4kg (3lb) carrots, peeled
rind of 2 lemons
50g (2oz) butter
30ml (2tbsp) sugar
2 cloves garlic, skinned and crushed
salt and pepper
chopped fresh parsley and blanched lemon shreds to garnish

1 Cut the carrots on the slant into thin slices. Peel and shred the rind of ½ a lemon. Blanch and drain, then reserve the shreds for the garnish.

2 Place the carrots in a saucepan with the remaining peeled lemon rind, the butter, sugar, garlic and seasoning. Just cover with cold water.

3 Bring to the boil, then cook over a moderate heat for about 12 minutes or until the carrots are tender and all the liquid has evaporated. Shake the pan to prevent the carrots from sticking. Garnish to serve.

NOT SUITABLE FOR FREEZING
SERVES 10-12

BREAD SAUCE

3 cloves
1 large onion, skinned
1.1 litres (2 pints) full-cream or semi-skimmed milk
2 bay leaves
salt and pepper
about 225g (8oz) fresh breadcrumbs
25g (1oz) butter

1 Stick the cloves into the onion. Place in a pan with the milk, bay leaves and seasoning. Bring to the boil; remove from the heat, cover and leave to infuse for about 30 minutes.

2 Remove the onion and bay leaves. Add the breadcrumbs and bring to the boil, stirring. Simmer for about 2-3 minutes. Stir in the butter, then adjust the seasoning. Keep warm in a covered dish. Stir before serving.

TO FREEZE:
Cool, pack and freeze.

TO USE:
Thaw overnight at cool room temperature. Reheat on top of the stove, adding extra milk if necessary.
SERVES 10-12

THE ALTERNATIVE TURKEY

What do you make on Christmas Day if there are only four of you – and you still want turkey, with lots of delicious accompaniments? Or what do you serve to a huge family gathering that will be spectacular, easy to serve (ie no tricky carving to serve the fifteenth member with something other than slices of legs and wings), and will not take hours to prepare and cook? The answers are the following two menus. The first, Turkey and Watercress Roulades served with Mixed Rice Pilaff and Glazed Carrots with Turnips, looks and tastes delicious and the meat dish can be made ahead and frozen.

The second menu will serve up to twenty, if you double up on the two salads – Chilled Potato Salad and Spiced Ratatouille Salad – with a spectacular cold Ballontine of

Turkey, filled with a loin of smoked pork, as the centrepiece. You will need a boned turkey to make this dish, but if you give plenty of warning, most butchers can do this for you. There are instructions for boning the bird yourself though. You can, if you prefer, serve the Ballontine hot, accompanied with the same sauces and vegetables as for the Glazed Stuffed Turkey on page 100.

TURKEY AND WATERCRESS ROULADES

1 bunch watercress
75g (3oz) Brazil nuts
65g (2½oz) butter or margarine
7.5ml (1½tsp) ground cumin
1 clove garlic, skinned and crushed
225g (8oz) full-fat soft cheese
finely grated rind and juice of 1 lemon
salt and pepper
700g (1½lb) turkey breast steaks (escalopes)
30ml (2tbsp) plain white flour
15ml (1tbsp) oil
300ml (½ pint) turkey or chicken stock
100ml (4fl oz) dry vermouth
30ml (2tbsp) single cream
watercress sprigs or chopped watercress to garnish
Mixed Rice Pilaff and Glazed Carrots with Turnips to accompany

1 Rinse and drain the watercress, then finely chop. Roughly chop the Brazil nuts.

2 Heat 40g (1½oz) of the butter in a frying pan. Add the nuts, cumin and garlic and stir-fry until beginning to brown. Mix in the watercress and stir-fry until all excess moisture has been driven off. Turn out into a bowl. Leave to cool.

3 Beat the watercress mixture together with the cheese and lemon rind. Season, cover and chill.

4 Meanwhile, place the turkey breast steaks between sheets of cling film. Bat out until very thin. Cut them up into ten to twelve even-sized pieces.

5 Divide the stuffing mixture among the turkey steaks. Roll up and secure with wooden cocktail sticks. Sprinkle the rolls with seasoned flour.

6 Heat the oil with the remaining butter in a shallow flameproof casserole. Brown the turkey rolls about half at a time. Remove from the casserole.

7 Stir any remaining flour into the pan juices. Pour in the stock and vermouth and bring to the boil. Season and stir in 15ml (1tbsp) lemon juice. Return the turkey rolls.

8 Cover and bake at 180°C (350°F) mark 4 for about 35 minutes or until the turkey is tender. Lift out the rolls and remove the cocktail sticks. Cover and keep warm.

9 Strain the cooking juices and boil to reduce slightly. Take off the heat, stir in the cream and adjust the seasoning. Halve the turkey rolls, spoon over a little of the sauce and serve the remainder separately. Garnish. Serve with Mixed Rice Pilaff and Glazed Carrots with Turnips.

TO FREEZE:
Cool, pack and freeze with the juices after baking.

TO USE:
Thaw overnight at cool room temperature. Cover and bake at 200°C (400°F) mark 6 for about 30 minutes, then complete in 9.
SERVES 4

A delicious alternative to roast turkey – Turkey and Watercress Roulades served with Mixed Rice Pilaff and Glazed Carrots with Turnips.

MIXED RICE PILAFF

If you cannot find the rice mix, use about 300g (11oz) long-grain white rice to 50g (2oz) wild rice – parboil the wild rice first until nearly tender.

75g (3oz) no-soak dried apricots
45ml (3tbsp) olive oil
1 bunch spring onions, trimmed and roughly chopped
225g (8oz) courgettes, sliced
375g (13oz) packet long grain and wild rice mixed
about 750ml (1¼ pints) stock
75ml (3 fl oz) dry vermouth
salt and pepper

1 Snip the apricots into strips. Heat the oil in a medium flameproof casserole. Add the onions, courgettes, apricots and rice and stir over a moderate heat for 2-3 minutes.
2 Pour in the stock and vermouth, season and bring to the boil. Cover and simmer gently for about 20 minutes or until the liquid has been absorbed and the rice is quite tender. Add a little more stock, if necessary.
3 Adjust seasoning. Cover and keep warm.

NOT SUITABLE FOR FREEZING
SERVES 4

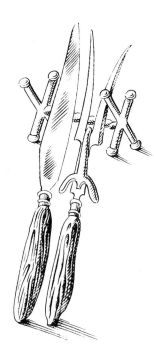

GLAZED CARROTS WITH TURNIPS

450g (1lb) carrots, peeled
450g (1lb) turnips, peeled
25g (1oz) butter or margarine, plus extra for serving
15ml (1tbsp) lemon juice
30ml (2tbsp) granulated sugar
salt and pepper

1 Cut the carrots and turnips into thick strips.
2 Place in a medium saucepan and *just* cover with cold water. Add 25g (1oz) butter, the lemon juice, sugar and season to taste.
3 Bring to the boil, boil over a high heat for about 15 minutes or until all liquid has evap-

orated and the vegetables are tender and lightly glazed. Shake the pan to prevent the vegetables sticking.
4 Cover and keep warm until required. Grind over black pepper to serve. Add an extra knob of butter, if wished.

NOT SUITABLE FOR FREEZING
SERVES 4

BALLONTINE OF TURKEY

It takes time (about 30 minutes) to bone the turkey but, fortunately, it can be done a day or two before the Christmas rush; carving is then much easier. Reserve all bones to make stock. The most important thing is not to puncture the skin, and to completely enclose the stuffing before roasting the ballontine. Trim away some of the turkey flesh before cooking to make a more slender version; you need enough flesh to wrap right around the loin of pork. The ballontine can be pressed lightly after cooking and while cooling to make it easier to slice: you may prefer not to press it to retain a well-rounded joint.

5.5kg (12lb) oven-ready turkey
butter or margarine
225g (8oz) onion, skinned and roughly chopped
225g (8oz) button mushrooms, roughly chopped
2 large cloves garlic, skinned and crushed
700g (1½lb) pork sausagemeat
125g (4oz) fresh breadcrumbs
90ml (6tbsp) chopped fresh parsley
60ml (4tbsp) Dijon mustard
grated rind and juice of 2 lemons
1 egg, beaten
salt and pepper
450g (1lb) smoked loin of pork (see Note)
Chilled Potato Salad, Spiced Ratatouille Salad, cranberry sauce with added apple and a salad of mixed leaves to accompany

1 First bone the turkey. Place the bird breast-side down on a large chopping board. Using a small sharp knife, cut straight along the backbone. Gradually fillet the flesh away from the carcass, keeping the knife as close to the bones as possible. Take great care not to puncture the skin as it has to act as a 'case' for the turkey roast – if the skin is split, the stuffing will burst out as the joint roasts.

2 Loosen the leg and wing ball-and-socket joints with the point of the knife. Push these joints away from the carcass until they loosen and partially come away. Carefully split the leg flesh and ease out the bones and sinews. Ease out the large wing joint, reserving the small wing tips for the stock pot. Run your fingers all over the turkey flesh to ensure there are no bones or sinews remaining.

3 You should have a large oblong of skin covered with turkey meat. Remove the parson's nose. Fillet most of the leg and thigh meat from *one side* of the bird and trim any excessively fat portions of breast flesh – you should have about 900g (2lb) trimmed meat to freeze and use in casseroles. (It is not essential to trim this flesh, but without it the ballontine will have a better shape, with even distribution of both turkey meat and stuffing.) Cover and refrigerate the boned turkey while preparing the stuffing.

4 Heat 50g (2oz) butter in a sauté pan, add the onion and fry until beginning to brown. Increase the heat, mix in the mushrooms and garlic and fry until all excess liquid has evaporated. Stir frequently. Turn into a large bowl and cool.

5 Stir the sausagemeat, breadcrumbs, parsley, mustard, lemon rind and 30ml (2tbsp) lemon juice, the egg and plenty of seasoning into the mushroom mixture. Beat well to combine thoroughly.

6 Lay the boned turkey flat on a board, flesh side up, and spread this stuffing mixture over the flesh. Place the smoked loin (cut in half lengthways if necessary – see Note) on top and then fold the turkey skin around to enclose the stuffing completely. Secure with fine skewers or cocktail sticks, or sew the skin together.

7 Spread the turkey generously with butter and season liberally with black pepper. Wrap in foil and place in a roasting tin.

8 Bake at 180°C (350°F) mark 4 for 2½ hours. Fold back the foil and return to the oven for 1 hour or until well browned. Test with a fine skewer, if it is cooked, the juices should run clear.

9 Lift the ballontine on to a serving plate. Either cool for about 20 minutes before slicing thickly to serve with the same accompaniments as for the Glazed Stuffed Turkey on page 100. Alternatively, cool completely, cover and chill before slicing to serve with Chilled Potato Salad, Spiced Ratatouille Salad, a salad of mixed leaves and cranberry sauce with added chopped apple.

TO FREEZE:
To serve cold only, cool, pack and freeze once completely cold.

TO USE:
Thaw overnight at cool room temperature.
SERVES ABOUT 20

CHILLED POTATO SALAD

1.4kg (3lb) old even-sized potatoes
salt and pepper
45ml (3tbsp) olive oil
45ml (3tbsp) grapeseed oil
45ml (3tbsp) lemon juice
75ml (5tbsp) mayonnaise
200ml (7fl oz) Greek-style natural yogurt
75ml (5tbsp) fresh snipped chives or spring onion tops (optional)
1 small bunch radishes, thinly sliced

1 Boil the potatoes, unpeeled, until tender. Peel and cut into large chunks. Keep warm.
2 Whisk together the oils, lemon juice, mayonnaise, yogurt and seasoning. Stir in most of the chives, if using.
3 Stir the dressing through the potatoes, being careful not to break them up. Cool, cover and chill well.
4 To serve: leave at cool room temperature for about 30 minutes. Stir gently and add the radishes and remainder of the chives.

NOT SUITABLE FOR FREEZING
SERVES 10-12

Note

Smoked loin of pork is available in the chiller cabinet of most large supermarkets. It is cooked and smoked and usually the shape of salami. If bought as a square, cut into oblongs before using as stuffing. You could use cooked ham, shaping it like a sausage.

SPICED RATATOUILLE SALAD

For maximum flavour, cook the vegetables until soft and mushy.

450g (1lb) aubergines, roughly chopped
salt and pepper
450g (1lb) fresh tomatoes, skinned
45ml (3tbsp) olive oil
225g (8oz) onion, skinned and roughly chopped
1 green pepper, seeded and chopped
1 red pepper, seeded and chopped
2.5ml (½tsp) chilli powder
2 cloves garlic, skinned and crushed
450g (1lb) courgettes, sliced
400g (14oz) can chopped tomatoes
5ml (1tsp) dried oregano
2 bay leaves
15ml (1tbsp) vinegar

1 Place the aubergine in a colander, sprinkle with salt and leave to stand for about 20 minutes. Rinse, drain and dry on absorbent kitchen paper.

2 Quarter and seed the tomatoes, reserving the juice; roughly chop the flesh.

3 Heat the oil in a large flameproof casserole. Add the onion, aubergine, peppers and chilli powder and stir-fry over a high heat for 2-3 minutes.

4 Mix in the garlic and all the remaining ingredients. Bring to the boil, cover and simmer for 30-40 minutes or until all the vegetables are soft and the liquid reduced. Adjust seasoning.

5 Cool, then chill well before serving.

TO FREEZE:
Pack and freeze.

TO USE:
Thaw overnight at cool room temperature. Chill again before serving.
SERVES 10-12

This Ballontine of Turkey will serve up to 20 people. Chilled Potato Salad and Spiced Ratatouille Salad make ideal accompaniments.

VEGETARIAN LUNCH FOR FOUR

What celebratory meal can you prepare for vegetarians? An omelette, nut roast or heavy pulse stew scarcely fit the bill, but what about delicious, tangy Stilton and Pear Flans, followed by a Lentil Roulade with Mushrooms, rounded off with a juicy Christmas Fruit Compote or a Frozen Christmas Pudding? Definitely good enough to serve up on Christmas Day, or at any dinner party.

Most of the dishes can be made ahead and frozen, but note that the Green Bean Salad will discolour once mixed with its dressing, so toss it lightly at the last minute.

Quantities for the puddings are for eight, not four, but you could make the full amount to allow for generous seconds. Alternatively, simply eat up the compote the following day, or freeze half the frozen pudding for another meal.

COUNTDOWN

ONE MONTH AHEAD: If wished, freeze recipes or ingredients as directed including the Frozen Christmas Pudding (see page 89). Make a note of thawing instructions.

ABOUT A WEEK AHEAD: Make a shopping list. Bake the pastry cases blind; cool and store in an airtight container.

TWO DAYS AHEAD: Prepare the Lentil Roulade to the end of step 3, cover and refrigerate. Prepare the Swiss roll tin; store, covered, in a cool place. Make the Green Bean Salad, cover and refrigerate (do not boil the egg yet). Prepare the Christmas Fruit Compote (see p 90), cover and chill.

CHRISTMAS EVE: Prepare the cheese custard for the pear flans. Slice the mushrooms and refrigerate in a polythene bag. Hardboil the egg for the salad; cool under running water, then refrigerate in a bowl of water. Rinse and drain salad ingredients of your choice. Dry well and refrigerate in polythene bags. Make a French dressing.

CHRISTMAS DAY: TO SERVE AT 1.30PM

ABOUT 12.30PM: Preheat the oven to 180°C (350°F) mark 4. Complete the pear flans and bake. Once they are baked, raise the oven temperature to 200°C (400°F) mark 6.

1.15PM: Take the Green Bean Salad out of the refrigerator and garnish with chopped egg. Beat the egg yolks into the Lentil Roulade, whisk the whites, complete and bake. Prepare the mushroom sauce, keep warm over a low heat.

1.30PM: Serve the starter.

ABOUT 1.45PM: Turn out and roll up the roulade and serve. Toss the Leafy Salad ingredients with the dressing. Reheat the compote if wished.

STILTON AND PEAR FLANS

75g (3oz) plain wholemeal flour
75g (3oz) plain white flour
75g (3oz) soft, tub margarine
5ml (1tsp) Dijon mustard
1 egg
60ml (4tbsp) milk
60ml (4tbsp) single cream
125g (4oz) blue Stilton cheese, grated
black pepper
2 small ripe pears

1 Mix together the flours in a bowl then, using a fork, cut in the margarine and mustard until evenly mixed. Add about 45ml (3tbsp) water and mix to a soft dough. Knead lightly, roll out thinly and use to line four 11.5cm (4½ inch) metal flan cases. Bake blind at 180°C (350°F) mark 4 until set.
2 Meanwhile, whisk together the egg, milk and cream. Stir in the cheese and plenty of pepper. Peel the pears, halve and, using a teaspoon, scoop out the core. Place each pear half flat-side down and slice crossways into thin strips.

3 Carefully place a pear half in each flan case, fanning out the strips. Spoon the cheese mixture around.

4 Bake at 180°C (350°F) mark 4 for 15-20 minutes or until the cheese mixture is just set and golden brown. Allow to cool for about 30 minutes before serving.

TO FREEZE:

Pack and freeze the baked pastry cases.

TO USE:

Thaw for 2-3 hours; complete as in 2.

LENTIL ROULADE WITH MUSHROOMS

175g (6oz) red lentils
450ml (¾ pint) vegetable stock
100g (4oz) onions, skinned and sliced
568ml (1 pint) milk
bay leaves, slices carrot and onion to flavour
75g (3oz) butter
60ml (4tbsp) flour
1 bunch watercress, rinsed
salt and pepper
Parmesan cheese
3 eggs, separated
225g (8oz) button mushrooms, sliced
30ml (2tbsp) lemon juice

1 Place the lentils in a sieve, then rinse under cold running water. Put in a small saucepan and pour in the stock. Add the onions and bring to the boil. Cover and simmer until the lentils are soft and all the liquid is absorbed – about 20 minutes. Stir occasionally to prevent the lentils sticking and boil off any remaining liquid at the end; cool slightly.

2 Meanwhile, bring the milk to the boil in a pan with the flavouring ingredients. Remove from the heat, cover and infuse for about 20 minutes. Melt 25g (1oz) of the butter in a small saucepan, stir in 30ml (2tbsp) of the flour followed by 200ml (7fl oz) strained, infused milk. Bring to the boil and cook for a couple of minutes, stirring.

3 In a food processor, blend together the lentils, sauce, watercress and plenty of seasoning. Blend until the lentils are almost smooth and the watercress finely chopped. Turn into a large bowl and leave until *completely* cold, refrigerating for 2-3 hours.

4 Meanwhile, grease and base-line a 23 × 33cm (9 × 13 inch) Swiss roll tin. Grease the paper and dust with Parmesan.

5 Beat the egg yolks into the lentil mixture. Whisk the whites until stiff but not dry, then fold into the mixture. Spread in the tin.

6 Bake at 200°C (400°F) mark 6 for 30 minutes or until well risen, and golden brown.

7 Meanwhile, quickly cook the mushrooms for 1-2 minutes in 50g (2oz) butter. Stir in the remaining flour followed by the remaining strained milk. Bring to the boil and cook, stirring for 1-2 minutes. Add the lemon juice and season. Keep warm over a low heat.

8 Have ready a large sheet of nonstick or greaseproof paper or foil sprinkled with Parmesan cheese. Flip the roulade over on to the paper and peel off the lining paper. Roll up immediately from the shortest end with the help of the sheet of paper. Lift on to a serving dish and serve with the sauce.

NOT SUITABLE FOR FREEZING

GREEN BEAN SALAD

350g (12oz) French beans, trimmed
salt and pepper
30ml (2tbsp) sunflower oil
15ml (1tbsp) olive oil
finely grated rind and juice of 1 lemon
1 clove garlic, skinned and crushed
1 egg, hard-boiled and chopped

1 Halve the beans, then cook in a pan of boiling salted water for 3-4 minutes only.

2 Meanwhile whisk together the oils with the lemon rind, 15ml (1tbsp) lemon juice, the garlic and seasoning.

3 Drain the cooked beans and, while still warm, stir into the dressing. When cool, cover and refrigerate.

4 Take the salad out of the refrigerator 30 minutes before serving. Stir well and sprinkle over the chopped egg.

TO FREEZE:

Blanch and freeze the beans.

TO USE:

Cook from frozen.

Entertaining

CHRISTMAS AND NEW YEAR are the peak entertain-ing season. It is the time of year when family and friends of all ages – and tastes – get together. In the space of a few weeks you can find yourself organising more dinners, suppers and drinks parties than you would normally contemplate in six months. On top of all this, you are probably having to cope with your normal household routine plus preparations for Christmas itself. No wonder many people claim not to enjoy their own parties very much.

Entertaining does not have to be so stressful. The keys to success are planning and cunning.

Throwing a good party involves careful preparation and planning; the food is important, but so is the drink, having enough plates and glasses, and warning the neighbours about the noise.

Planning means you stay in control of events – making it far more likely you will actually enjoy the event. Cunning will save you time and energy: like doubling up on quantities if you have two parties in a row (admittedly tricky for large gatherings); or sticking to cold starters and puddings so you have only one main dish to cook. In this section are lots of expert tips and shortcuts to making your entertaining go more smoothly – and enjoyably.

MENUS

These take a lot of the panic out of planning your party – whatever the size and scale. Work out a good balance of flavours, textures and colours – appearance is just as important as taste. Avoid obvious mistakes like cream and butter in every course, or too many strong flavours in one course. If you are uncertain what your guests will and won't eat, stick to simple ingredients: most people enjoy some sort of salad, followed by a light chicken dish with crunchy vegetables, then a fruit tart, or just cheese and fruit. Don't be too elaborate unless you positively relish tricky techniques and last minute pyrotechnics in the kitchen. It is probably unrealistic to stick totally to old favourites over Christmas, so if you are embarking on a new recipe at least choose one which is simple to prepare and doesn't sound too outlandish. Ideally, have a dummy run with the family first.

Do bear in mind the limits of your refrigerator and oven, and the sizes of your cooking equipment. Soup for twelve needs a very large pan, while too many cold snacks could fill up your refrigerator leaving no room for cooling drinks – or the rest of your food. An oven crammed with casseroles won't work efficiently, so you may need to reassess your menu if you seem to have too many hot dishes to cook or reheat on the day. Finally, if you are serving a buffet or finger foods, do make sure the former can be eaten easily with a fork, the latter with fingers. It is not comfortable to have to perch with a knife and fork on a chair arm in order to eat, nor to have over-large snacks fall apart in your hands before they can reach your mouth.

PLANNING

Once you have decided on the menu, make a detailed timetable of what to do and buy and when. Pin it in a prominent place and tick things off as you go. The aim is to leave nothing out and prevent yourself duplicating purchases, like two lot of napkins. Also with so much else being bought at Christmas it is easy to forget what foods are for which meals: your list will help.

● Make a detailed shopping list of all foods and non foods (see Party Checklist, page 116) you need.
● Order drinks and glasses (see Drinks for Parties, page 156)
● Arrange extra help (see below).
● Hire tables, chairs, china and cutlery (see below).
● Book space in neighbours refrigerators and freezers if you need to.
● Write a detailed timetable of when to prepare each recipe, reheat it and garnish it.
● Order flowers if required.

EXTRA HELP

Professional waiters, waitresses and butlers are a real help at large gatherings. They usually take guests' coats, serve food and drink, and may wash up afterwards. Check first though. You can hire help through local agencies which advertise in Yellow Pages or other commercial directories. Do brief them on what is to be served when, and familiarise them with the kitchen. As a rule of thumb, a professional help can cope with twenty-five guests, untrained fifteen. Do book early as agencies tend to be busy.

HIRING EQUIPMENT

Yellow pages will list under Catering Equipment Hire or Wedding Services. If there is no extra charge, order the equipment a day in advance so you can check it first, and wash it if necessary (it may be dusty). Some firms take equipment back dirty – this tends to add to the cost but certainly saves time. Run through your menu and guest list checking what you will need and how many (see Party Checklist).

QUANTITY CHART

Below are approximate quantities to serve 12 people. For 25 people, multiply the quantities by two. For 50 people multiply by four. For 75 people multiply by five and a half. For 100 people multiply by seven.

Cocktail Eats
Allow about 80 small eats for 12 people to serve before a meal
Allow about 120 small eats for 12 people to serve alone

Starters
Soups – allow 2.6 litres (4½ pints) for 12
Pâtés – allow 1.1kg (2½ lb) for 12
Smoked salmon – allow 900g (2lb) for 12
Prawns – 900g (2lb) for 12

Main Dishes
Boneless chicken or turkey – allow 1.8kg (4lb) for 12
Whole chicken – allow three 1.4kg (3lb) oven ready birds for 12
Turkey – allow one 5.5kg (12lb) oven ready bird for 12
Lamb/beef/pork:
boneless – allow 2-2.3kg (4½-5lb) for 12
on the bone – allow 3.2-3.6kg (7-8lb) for 12
mince – allow 2kg (4½lb) for 12

Fish
Whole with head – allow 2.3kg (5lb) for 12
Steaks – allow twelve 175g (6oz) steaks for 12
Fillets – allow 2kg (4½lb) for 12
Prawns – allow 1.4kg (3lb) for 12 (main course)

Accompaniments
Potatoes:
roast and mashed – allow 2kg (4½lb) for 12
new – allow 1.8kg (4lb) for 12

Rice and pasta – allow 700g (1½lb) for 12

Green vegetables – allow 1.4kg (3lb) for 12

(for fresh spinach allow about 3.6kg (8lb) for 12)

Salads
Tomatoes – allow 700g (1½lb) for 12
Salad leaves – allow 2 medium heads for 12
Cucumber – allow 1 large for 12

French dressing – allow 175ml (6fl oz) for 12
Mayonnaise – allow 300ml (½ pint) for 12

Bread
Fresh bread – allow 1 large loaf for 12
Medium sliced bread – allow 1 large loaf for 12 (about 24 slices)

Cheeses
For a wine and cheese party – allow 1.4kg (3lb) for 12
To serve at the end of a meal – allow 700g (1½lb) for 12

Butter
To serve with bread or biscuits and cheese – allow 225g (8oz) for 12
To serve with bread and biscuits and cheese – allow 350g (12oz) for 12

For sandwiches – allow 175g (6oz) softened butter for 12 rounds

Cream
For pudding or dessert – allow 600ml (1 pint) single cream for 12
For coffee – allow 300ml (½ pint) single cream for 12

Milk
Allow 450ml (15fl oz) for 12 cups of tea

Coffee and Tea
Ground coffee – allow about 125g (4oz) for 12 medium cups
Instant – allow about 75g (3oz) for 12 large cups
Tea – allow about 25g (1oz) for 12 medium cups

COOKING IN QUANTITY

The dynamics of cooking large quantities are more complicated than simply quadrupling your favourite recipe. Liquids will not reduce at the same speed, leaving you with watery casseroles and sunken cakes. Unless you are an experienced caterer, do not attempt to cook recipes for more than twelve people at one time. Few casserole dishes or saucepans will hold more than this. Instead, cook food in smaller batches and chill or freeze.

LAYING OUT THE BUFFET

Have several serving points for the buffet food and the drinks too. This avoids bottle-necks and long delays. Ensure that plates, cutlery and napkins are set out at the start of the buffet table. Don't pile serving platters too high or food will spill over the table. It is better to replenish the dishes as necessary. Keep food tightly covered until it is served and if possible add garnishes at the last minute too. They will look freshest then. Portion pies and gâteaux before the buffet starts or station one of the helpers to serve them out as guests are often loath to be the first one to cut into them. And do ensure that there are some seats available.

PARTY HINTS

● Make sure you have plenty of rubbish bags and drying up cloths for the clearing and washing up afterwards.
● Decide where to stack dirty plates if you are holding a large party. A separate table or sideboard is a good idea.
● Serve colourless drinks such as white wine, lemonade, champagne, mineral water, white vermouth or gin to eliminate possible stains on your carpets and rugs.
● For the same reason, steer clear of foods likely to stain permanently such as red berry fruits, curry and beetroot.
● Don't mop up any spills with coloured paper napkins as they are likely to stain the underlying surface.
● Make lots of ice cubes in advance, and store them in freezer plastic bags in the freezer. First, spray them with soda water so they don't stick together.
● For formal meals, make sure you only have to cook one course on the actual day.
● For large sit down gatherings, use place cards to prevent searching for seats.
● Keep flower arrangements and candles on tables low, so people can see and talk over them.
● Use a fragrant candle to mask the smell of tobacco and cigar smoke.
● Keep lighting soft, music low, to relax guests.
● Warn the neighbours if you are expecting a crowd and guests are likely to be noisy and hog parking spaces.

A perfect antidote to turkey: a light supper for six of rolled plaice and smoked salmon with a light leek sauce, crisp vegetable bake, steamed cauliflower with artichoke hearts and black olives.

PARTY CHECKLIST

Tick off the items below as you acquire them.

ashtrays	drink	matches
bin liners for rubbish	flowers	napkins
bottle stoppers	forks	plates
bowls	glasses	servers
candles	hand towels	serving dishes
candleholders	heated trolley/tray	soap
coat hangers	ice/ice buckets	spoons
coffee cups	jugs	table cloths
corkscrews	knives	table mats
crown cap openers	lemons	tissues
disposable tableware	loo paper	

PARTY SNACKS FOR 30 – 35 GUESTS

Most of these savouries can be made ahead and frozen, with just a few to make the day before or on the day. Allow about eight snacks per person, but if you are uncertain of numbers and appetites, provide a cheeseboard, French bread and a bowl of fruit as standby. Or, as an alternative, prepare or buy sticks of celery, cucumber and other crudités and serve with tubs of taramasalata, mackerel pâté and soft cheese with garlic.

PARTY SNACKS FOR 30-35

Small Crab Cakes

Tomato and Yogurt Dip

Salmon and Prawn Flan

Baked Bacon Sticks with Cheese and Garlic Dip

Crisp Caraway Biscuits

Cheesy Bread Twists

Filo Sausage Rolls

Marinated Mushrooms

COUNTDOWN

UP TO 1 WEEK AHEAD: Make the Crisp Caraway Biscuits, store in an airtight container. Make the Tomato and Yogurt Dip. Cover and store in the refrigerator.

TWO DAYS AHEAD: Make the Small Crab Cakes, Filo Sausage Rolls and the Cheesy Bread Twists. Store in the refrigerator as directed. Shop for extra cheeses and fruit, which you may need to serve if unexpected guests arrive.

THE DAY BEFORE: Make the Salmon and Prawn Flan. Cool, cover and refrigerate. Make the Marinated Mushrooms. Cool, cover and refrigerate. Cook and cool the potatoes for the Baked Bacon Sticks; wrap with bacon. Wrap the mushrooms with the bacon. Cover and refrigerate. Cut the vegetable crudités for the Tomato and Yogurt Dip; store in separate polythene bags in the refrigerator. Peel and cut up any extra vegetables you are planning to use for latecomers; cover and refrigerate.

TO SERVE FOR LUNCH OR DINNER
2 HOURS BEFORE: Place the dips in two separate serving dishes, cover and refrigerate. Place the Small Crab Cakes, Filo Sausage Rolls, Cheesy Bread Twists and Crisp Caraway Biscuits on separate baking sheets. Cover loosely with foil ready to reheat. Place the savoury Bacon Sticks in a roasting tin. Prepare the cheese board and fruit platter if you are having one.

1 HOUR BEFORE: Reheat the Salmon and Prawn Flan. Cool before cutting up into triangles or diamonds. Refresh the Crisp Caraway Biscuits. Arrange the crudités on serving plates. Take out the Marinated Mushrooms and arrange on a platter with cocktail sticks.

30 MINUTES BEFORE: Cook a sheet of Baked Bacon Sticks and reheat some crab cakes, sausage rolls and bread twists. Do not reheat all at once, as you will probably want to serve some warm items later in the afternoon or evening.

SMALL CRAB CAKES

These are delicious served warm.

125g (4oz) self-raising white flour
2.5ml (½tsp) baking powder
pinch salt
50g (2oz) butter or margarine
125g (4oz) white crab meat, flaked
1 egg
about 30ml (2tbsp) milk
5ml (1tsp) fresh dill or large pinch dried dill weed
white vegetable fat
15ml (1tbsp) grated Parmesan cheese

1 Sift together the flour, baking powder and salt into a bowl. Rub in the butter until the mixture resembles breadcrumbs. Stir in the crab meat.
2 Whisk the egg with the milk and dill. Add to the flour mixture and stir to form a smooth, thick batter, adding a little more milk if necessary.
3 Brush a biscuit tin or mini mince pie tins with melted white vegetable fat and spoon in the batter mixture to almost fill. Sprinkle lightly with Parmesan cheese.
4 Bake at 200°C (400°F) mark 6 for about 10-12 minutes or until well risen and golden. Remove from the tins and allow to

cool slightly. Serve warm. Store in a poly-thene bag in the refrigerator for up to two days; refresh in a warm oven before serving.

TO FREEZE:
Pack and freeze.

TO USE:
Thaw overnight at cool room temperature. Place on baking sheets, cover loosely with foil and reheat in a moderate oven.
SERVES 40

TOMATO AND YOGURT DIP

10ml (2tsp) pink peppercorns in brine
300ml (½ pint) Greek style natural yogurt
60ml (4tbsp) tomato purée
salt and pepper
vegetable crudités, to serve

1 Crush the peppercorns and mix with the yogurt and tomato purée. Season to taste.
2 Serve in a small bowl surrounded by a selection of vegetables crudités or Baked Bacon Sticks. Store the dip, covered, in the refrigerator for up to a week; stir before serving.

NOT SUITABLE FOR FREEZING
SERVES 12

SALMON AND PRAWN FLAN

Serve this rich creamy flan cut into small pieces.

450g (1lb) plain white flour
salt and pepper
275g (10oz) butter or margarine
450g (1lb) full-fat soft cheese
450ml (15fl oz) double cream
6 eggs
45ml (3tbsp) chopped fresh chervil or parsley
225g (8oz) cooked peeled prawns
225g (8oz) salmon fillet, skinned
cooked peeled prawns and fresh dill, if available, to garnish

1 Sift the flour with a large pinch of salt into a medium bowl. Rub or fork in the butter until the mixture resembles fine bread-crumbs. Mix in 90-120ml (6-8tbsp) cold water and knead lightly to make a firm dough. Wrap and chill for about 15 minutes.
2 Roll out half the pastry at a time and use to line two 32×22cm (12½×8½ inch) Swiss roll tins. Prick the bases with a fork.
3 Bake blind at 200°C (400°F) mark 6 for about 10 minutes. Remove the paper and beans and return to the oven for another 10 minutes or until the bases have dried out and turned golden brown.
4 Meanwhile, blend or beat together the cheese, cream, eggs and herbs. Season well. Roughly chop the prawns. Cut the salmon into small 0.5cm (¼ inch) cubes.
5 Arrange the salmon and prawns in the flan cases; pour over the cheese and egg mix-ture.
6 Place on baking sheets and bake at 190°C (375°F) mark 5 for about 30 minutes or until set and well browned. Swop the positions of the tins halfway through cooking. Allow to cool completely. Cover and refrigerate for up to one day. Cover loosely and refresh in a moderate oven for about 20 minutes. Cut into neat triangles or diamonds for serv-ing. Garnish with cooked peeled prawns and fresh dill.

NOT SUITABLE FOR FREEZING
MAKES ABOUT 100 PIECES

BAKED BACON STICKS

These are delicious served with the cheese and garlic dip. Canadian-style streaky bacon, which has been maple cured, has a delicious flavour and becomes crisp and golden on cooking. The dip may also be served with vegetable crudités.

700g (1½lb) small new potatoes
900g (2lb) Canadian-style streaky bacon
450g (1lb) mushrooms, brown cap or cup
300ml (½ pint) Greek-style natural yogurt
225g (8oz) low-fat soft cheese
1 clove garlic, skinned and crushed
salt and pepper
15ml (1tbsp) snipped fresh chives to garnish

Cheesy Bread Twists, Crisp Caraway Biscuits, Baked Bacon Sticks and Filo Sausage Rolls are perfect snacks for a drinks party. The twists, biscuits and sausage rolls can be frozen in advance.

1 Wash but do not peel the potatoes. Cut any large ones in half. Steam or boil until tender, about 8 minutes.

2 Meanwhile, remove the bacon rind and stretch each rasher with the back of a knife. Cut each rasher in half. Halve any large mushrooms.

3 Wrap the cut bacon rashers around the potatoes and mushrooms. Cover and refrigerate for up to one day.

4 Place in roasting tins or on baking sheets. Bake at 200°C (400°F) mark 6 for about 15 minutes or until crisp and golden. Spear with cocktail sticks to serve.

5 Meanwhile, mix together the yogurt, soft cheese, garlic and seasoning. Place in a small serving bowl and garnish with snipped chives. Arrange the bacon rolls around the dip.

NOT SUITABLE FOR FREEZING
MAKES ABOUT 60

CRISP CARAWAY BISCUITS

The strong flavour of caraway seeds complements the cheese perfectly in these crisp biscuits. The biscuit dough may be shaped into various attractive shapes – squares, triangles, circles or ovals, whichever you prefer.

350g (12oz) plain white flour
7.5ml (1½tsp) salt
7.5ml (1½tsp) dry mustard powder
175g (6oz) butter or margarine
350g (12oz) mature Gouda or Cheddar cheese, finely grated
3 eggs, beaten
caraway seeds to sprinkle

1 Sift the flour, salt and mustard powder into a medium bowl. Rub or fork in the butter until the mixture resembles breadcrumbs. Add the cheese.

2 Reserve a little egg for glazing. Stir the rest into the flour mixture. Bring the mixture together to form a soft dough. Wrap the pastry and chill for about 15 minutes.

3 Roll out the pastry to a thickness of about 0.5cm (¼ inch). Cut out squares, triangles, circles or ovals – about 4cm (1½ inches) in size.

4 Place on baking sheets, brush with the remaining egg, then sprinkle with caraway seeds. Knead the pastry trimmings and re-roll once only. Repeat the cutting and glazing process.

5 Bake at 200°C (400°F) mark 6 for about 10 minutes or until crisp and golden. Transfer the biscuits on to a wire rack to cool. Store in an airtight container for up to 1 week.

TO FREEZE:

Pack and freeze.

TO USE:

Thaw overnight at cool room temperature. Place on baking sheets and refresh in a hot oven.

MAKES ABOUT 40

CHEESY BREAD TWISTS

125g (4oz) butter or margarine
150ml (¼ pint) milk
2 eggs
350g (12oz) strong plain white flour
5ml (1tsp) fast-acting dried yeast
5ml (1tsp) salt
oil
125g (4oz) Gruyère cheese, finely grated
paprika
poppy seeds and/or sesame seeds

1 Melt the butter, allow to cool a little. Beat with the milk and one egg.

2 Place the flour, yeast and salt in a bowl. Make a well in the centre, add the milk mixture and beat steadily to form a smooth dough. Turn out on to a lightly floured work surface and knead until smooth, about 4-5 minutes.

3 Place in a lightly oiled bowl, cover with oiled cling film and leave to rise in a warm place for about 1 hour, or until doubled in size.

4 Knead the dough gently, then roll out into a rectangle to a thickness of about 0.5cm (¼ inch).

5 Brush half the dough with beaten egg, then sprinkle over the cheese. Fold the dough over to cover the filling completely. Roll out again to a thickness of 0.5cm (¼ inch).

6 Cut into strips 1cm (½ inch) wide and about 15cm (6 inches) long. Twist each strip several times and place on greased baking sheets. Brush lightly with egg, sprinkle with paprika and poppy and/or sesame seeds.

7 Bake at 220°C (425°F) mark 7 for 10 minutes or until golden. Serve warm or cold. Store in an airtight container for up to two days; refresh in a warm oven before serving.

TO FREEZE:

Pack and freeze.

TO USE:

Thaw overnight at cool room temperature. Place on baking sheets, cover loosely with foil and reheat in a moderate oven.

MAKES ABOUT 40

FILO SAUSAGE ROLLS

Choose a good quality herb sausage for extra flavour. Filo pastry makes a lighter case than puff or flaky.

450g (1lb) pork and herb sausages (about 9 sausages)

9 sheets filo pastry – 45.5×28cm (18×11 inches) in size

butter or margarine, melted

wholegrain mustard

lightly beaten egg and poppy seeds, to finish

1 Skin the sausages. Set aside. (This is easier if the sausages are well chilled before handling.)

2 Brush three sheets of filo pastry with melted butter, stacking them as you go. Keep the remaining pastry covered.

3 Place a sausage along the shorter side of the filo. Squeeze the sausage meat out to make it fit the width of the pastry. Spread over a little mustard to taste.

4 Roll the pastry over the sausage three or four times to use up one third of the length of the pastry. Cut the pastry to release the sausage. Brush the top with more melted butter, cut into four to six pieces and place on baking sheets.

5 Repeat with two more sausages until the first stack of pastry is used. Butter and stack three more sheets of filo and repeat steps 3 and 4. Repeat the process for the final three sheets of filo.

6 Brush with lightly beaten egg and sprinkle with poppy seeds. Bake at 200°C (400°F) mark 6 for about 20 minutes or until crisp

and golden. Cool. Refrigerate for up to two days, covered.

TO FREEZE:

Pack and freeze.

TO USE:

Thaw overnight at cool room temperature. Place on baking sheets, cover loosely with foil and reheat in a moderate oven.
MAKES 36-54, DEPENDING ON SIZE

MARINATED MUSHROOMS

The olives included in this recipe add extra flavour.

1.1kg (2½lb) small button mushrooms

5 cloves garlic, skinned and crushed

75ml (5tbsp) oil

600ml (1 pint) red wine

15ml (1tbsp) dried thyme

450g (1lb) stuffed green olives

salt and pepper

1 Sauté the mushrooms and garlic in the oil in batches, for about 2 minutes for each batch. Place the mushrooms in a large saucepan. Add the remaining ingredients and simmer until the wine is reduced by half. Cool.

2 Cover the mushrooms and olives, then chill. Drain. Serve with cocktail sticks.

NOT SUITABLE FOR FREEZING
SERVES ABOUT 40

DRINKS PARTY MENU FOR 24

There are some wonderful intense flavours in these snacks: coriander, pesto, chilli and curry. To balance them are the more classical tastes of cheese, smoked salmon and mushroom, so there really shouldn't be any dissatisfied guests. Again, most of the snacks can be frozen. For drink ideas, see Drinks for Parties on page 156.

COUNTDOWN

TWO WEEKS AHEAD: Prepare the Olives with Pesto, the Mixed Spice Nuts and the Herb Twists.

TWO DAYS AHEAD: Make the peanut sauce for the Pork Satay; cover and refrigerate. Prepare the Cheese and Peanut Butter Shorties including the quantity for the Smoked Salmon and Cheese Crisps. Refrigerate. Make the Smoked Salmon and Peppercorn filling, cover and refrigerate.

THE DAY BEFORE: Complete and refrigerate the Smoked Salmon and Cheese Crisps.

ON THE DAY: TO SERVE AT 12 NOON

9AM: Cut up and marinate the pork. Fill the Mushroom and Crab Canapés. Refrigerate.

11AM: Garnish the Smoked Salmon and Cheese Crisps. Take the peanut sauce out of the refrigerator. Arrange all the snacks on serving plates. Garnish the Mushroom and Crab Canapés. Grill the pork and spear on to cocktail sticks.

PORK SATAY

Serve the satay sauce cold or just warm as a dip for the pork or crudités.

450g (1lb) pork fillet
20ml (4tsp) mild curry powder
2.5ml (½tsp) ground coriander
2.5ml (½tsp) ground turmeric
2.5ml (½tsp) cayenne pepper
salt and pepper
45ml (3tbsp) sesame oil
50g (2oz) creamed coconut
125g (4oz) salted peanuts
30ml (2tbsp) granulated sugar
5ml (1tsp) lemon juice
Tabasco sauce

1 Cut the pork into small pieces to skewer on to cocktail sticks. Place in a shallow dish. Add 15ml (1tbsp) of the curry powder, the coriander, 1.25ml (¼tsp) of the turmeric, 1.25ml (¼tsp) of the cayenne pepper and seasoning. Knead the spices into the pork with 15ml (1tbsp) sesame oil and 5ml (1tsp) cold water. Cover, then refrigerate for about 2 hours.
2 Meanwhile for the sauce, finely chop the creamed coconut and dissolve in 150ml (¼ pint) boiling water.
3 Process the peanuts with 5ml (1tsp) curry powder, 1.25ml (¼tsp) turmeric, 1.25ml (¼tsp) cayenne pepper and the sugar until finely chopped. Add the coconut liquid, lemon juice, a few dashes of Tabasco and seasoning. Blend again.
4 Grill the pork under a medium heat until cooked through. Spear on cocktail sticks to serve hot or cold with the sauce.

TO FREEZE:
Pack and freeze the uncooked pork and sauce separately.

TO USE:
Thaw overnight at cool room temperature. Cook the pork as directed.
SERVES 6

DRINKS PARTY FOR 24

Pork Satay

Olives with Pesto

Mixed Spiced Nuts

Cheese and Peanut Shorties

Herb Twists

Mushroom and Crab Canapés

Smoked Salmon and Cheese Crisps

OLIVES WITH PESTO

Remember, you will need to start this recipe a week ahead of the party. Serve the olives as a cocktail snack or in salads. Alternatively, put them in pretty jars to make an unusual present. The oil can be used to enrich salad dressings.

1 green chilli
450g (1lb) black olives, preferably stoned
30ml (2tbsp) pesto sauce
300ml (½ pint) olive oil

1 Halve the chilli. Thinly slice the flesh, discarding the seeds. (It is advisable to wear rubber gloves while doing this, as chillies can irritate your skin.)
2 Mix together all the ingredients. Spoon into small jars and cover tightly with non-metallic lids. Refrigerate for at least one week.

NOT SUITABLE FOR FREEZING
SERVES ABOUT 10

MIXED SPICED NUTS

Stir the nuts frequently in the frying pan, because as they cook, they brown and quickly burn.

30ml (2tbsp) oil
40g (1½oz) butter
125g (4oz) blanched almonds
125g (4oz) unsalted cashew nuts
225g (8oz) unsalted peanuts in their skins
5ml (1tsp) chilli powder
salt

1 Heat the oil and butter in a large frying pan.
2 Add the nuts with half the chilli powder, then fry over a moderate heat, stirring frequently, until evenly browned.
3 Immediately spoon out on to absorbent kitchen paper. Dry slightly, then tip into a bowl and sprinkle with the remaining chilli powder and a little salt. Stir to mix.

4 Once cold, store in an airtight container until required.

TO FREEZE:
Pack and freeze.

TO USE:
Thaw, wrapped, for about 4 hours.
SERVES ABOUT 10

CHEESE AND PEANUT SHORTIES

These savoury biscuits simply melt in the mouth; they can be served with drinks or as a spicy and savoury accompaniment to soups and starters.

175g (6oz) plain white flour
2.5ml (½tsp) paprika pepper
175g (6oz) butter
175g (6oz) mature Cheddar cheese, grated
15ml (1tbsp) wholegrain mustard
1 egg, beaten
about 75g (3oz) unsalted peanuts, chopped

1 Mix the flour and paprika together. Rub in the butter until evenly mixed. Stir in the cheese and mustard; knead until just smooth.
2 On a well-floured work surface, roll out the mixture to about 0.5cm (¼ inch) thickness. Brush with beaten egg, then sprinkle with the chopped nuts.
3 Cut out the mixture into rounds, fingers or triangles and place on baking sheets. Knead and re-roll any trimmings, stamp out as before.
4 Bake at 180°C (350°F) mark 4 for about 15 minutes or until well browned and crisp. Cool on wire racks.
5 Store in an airtight container in the refrigerator.

TO FREEZE:
Pack and freeze.

TO USE:
Thaw for 2-3 hours.
MAKES ABOUT 30

HERB TWISTS

Fresh herbs can also be used in the mixture, if they are available.
(See Suppliers.)

65g (2½oz) butter, softened
40g (1½oz) full-fat soft cheese
1 egg yolk
175g (6oz) plain flour
salt
cayenne pepper
5ml (1tsp) dried tarragon
30ml (2tbsp) grated Parmesan cheese

1 Beat the butter, soft cheese and egg yolk together in a bowl, then stir in the flour sifted with a pinch of salt. Add a pinch of cayenne, the tarragon and 10ml (2tsp) water.
2 Knead lightly until smooth. Wrap and chill for 30 minutes.
3 Roll out the pastry thinly and cut into narrow strips about 7.5×0.5cm (3×¼ inch). Twist the strips and place on baking sheets, pressing the ends down well to prevent the strips unwinding. Sprinkle with Parmesan.
4 Bake at 180°C (350°F) mark 4 for about 15 minutes. Cool on wire racks and store in an airtight container for up to two weeks.

TO FREEZE:
Pack and freeze.

TO USE:
Thaw, then refresh in a hot oven.
MAKES ABOUT 70

MUSHROOM AND CRAB CANAPÉS

Replace the crabmeat with the same quantity of chopped prawns, if wished.

350g (12oz) small cup mushrooms (25-30)
170g (6oz) can white crabmeat or 175g (6oz) frozen white crabmeat
30ml (2tbsp) lemon mayonnaise
grated rind of 1 lemon
30ml (2tbsp) fresh chopped parsley
salt and pepper
caviar or lump fish caviar to garnish

1 Remove the mushroom stalks (use for stock).
2 Mix together the crabmeat, mayonnaise, lemon rind, parsley and seasoning.
3 Spoon into the mushroom cups. Chill before serving garnished with caviar.

NOT SUITABLE FOR FREEZING
MAKES ABOUT 25

SMOKED SALMON AND CHEESE CRISPS

Pipe and freeze ahead to save on last-minute preparation.

| 1 quantity Cheese and Peanut Shorties, omitting peanuts |
| 1 quantity Smoked Salmon and Peppercorn filling |
| smoked salmon pieces, fresh dill, lemon or cucumber strips, pink peppercorns, caviar or lump fish caviar, prawns to garnish |

1 Make up the Cheese and Peanut Shorties as directed but omit the peanuts. Bake and cool. Store in an airtight container.
2 Mix together the ingredients for Smoked Salmon and Peppercorn filling. (This will store in the refrigerator for two to three days.)
3 Allow the salmon and cheese mixture to come to room temperature. Place into a piping bag fitted with a 1cm (½ inch) rose nozzle. Pipe a rosette on to each biscuit. Garnish and serve.

NOT SUITABLE FOR FREEZING

SMOKED SALMON AND PEPPERCORN FILLING

| 10ml (2tsp) pink peppercorns in brine |
| 50g (2oz) smoked salmon, not previously frozen |
| 225g (8oz) full-fat soft cheese |
| 125g (4oz) unsalted butter, softened |
| 30ml (2tbsp) lemon juice |
| 60ml (4tbsp) single cream |

1 Finely chop the peppercorns and smoked salmon. Beat the soft cheese, butter, lemon juice and cream together in a bowl.
2 Beat in the peppercorns and smoked salmon. Chill for about 40 minutes.

NOT SUITABLE FOR FREEZING

Storing Food Safety

• Make sure all the hot dishes are thoroughly cooked before serving. Don't keep food hot for more than an hour before people eat it.
• Cover food that is likely to dry out, such as sliced meat. Leave food like roast potatoes uncovered, so they stay crisp and dry.
• Root vegetables will keep warm; it is harder to keep leaf spinach or cabbage warm successfully.
• Casseroles and chilli con carne are the kind of dishes that retain their heat well.
• Reheat cook-chill foods thoroughly before putting them on a hot tray or trolley.

GOURMET BANQUET FOR EIGHT

This would make a splendid Christmas day feast, or an elegant dinner party for special guests. Goose always used to be the favoured bird for Christmas, and many people still prefer its richer flavour to that of turkey. The one drawback to a goose is that it is not so generously covered with meat as turkey, so you won't get much in the way of useful leftovers. But goose fat, which has to be poured off the bird as it cooks, makes wonderful crisp roast potatoes and keeps well in the refrigerator. In this menu, the rich flavour of the goose is perfectly complemented by the tartness and sweetness of the olive and prune stuffing. The starter of Turbans of Prawn and Trout with Pink Peppercorn Sauce is a fabulous combination of flavours, colours and textures, and can be partly prepared ahead and frozen. The Diamond Potatoes, Baked Apple Moulds and Julienne of Courgettes look as good as they taste, and are worth the extra time to prepare. The pudding is a real party piece – crowns of puff pastry enclosing delicious fruit and cream – it looks spectacular and is surprisingly easy to make.

PREPARING A GOOSE FOR COOKING

Remove the neck, giblets and fat from the body cavity. Use the giblets (not the liver) to make a thin gravy. Rinse the goose under cold running water, letting the water run through the body cavity. Dry inside and out with absorbent kitchen paper.

COUNTDOWN

TWO DAYS AHEAD: Make the Parmesan and Rosemary Wafers, then store in an airtight container. Make the pastry crowns, then store in an airtight container. Make the raspberry purée, cover and keep chilled.

THE DAY BEFORE: Prepare the Bacon Twists, cover and refrigerate. Fillet the trout and prepare filling for the Turbans of Prawn and Trout with Pink Peppercorn Sauce. Cover and refrigerate separately. Infuse the wine and peppercorns for the sauce, cover and chill. Make the Quick Christmas Tree Rolls. Cool and store in polythene bags. Prepare the stuffing for the goose, cover and refrigerate. Peel the potatoes, cover with cold water and store in a cool place. Cut the courgettes into julienne strips, rinse in acidulated water, shake dry and refrigerate in a polythene bag.

ON THE DAY: TO SERVE AT 8.30PM

3.30PM: Preheat oven to 220°C (425°F) mark 7. Stuff the goose and put to roast. Slice the apples for the moulds, keep covered with cold, acidulated water. Completed the turbans but do not bake them yet. Whip the cream for the Raspberry Chantilly Crowns. Refrigerate.

6.00PM: Put the potatoes in to bake.

7.15PM: Bake the Turbans of Prawn and Trout with Pink Peppercorn Sauce. Bake the Bacon Twists. Steam the courgettes. Make the gravy. Put out the Parmesan and Rosemary Wafers and the Quick Christmas Tree Rolls. Assemble the dessert just before serving.

GOURMET BANQUET FOR 8

Parmesan and Rosemary Wafers

Bacon Twists

Quick Christmas Tree Rolls or Mini Cottage Loaves

Turbans of Prawn and Trout with Pink Peppercorn Sauce

Roast Goose Stuffed with Olives and Prunes

Baked Apple Moulds

Diamond Potatoes

Julienne of Courgettes

Raspberry Chantilly Crowns

Tip

After cooking a fatty bird like goose, wipe excess grease off the oven door as soon as it is cool enough to do so, and before the fat has a chance to harden. Do the same for your oven sides if they are not self-cleaning, and wash the shelves in hot soapy water.

PARMESAN AND ROSEMARY WAFERS

50g (2oz) softened unsalted butter or margarine
10ml (2tsp) caster sugar
white of 1 medium egg, size 5
2.5ml (½tsp) salt
90ml (6tbsp) plain white flour
30ml (2tbsp) grated Parmesan cheese
30ml (2tbsp) fresh rosemary sprigs or 15ml (1tbsp) dried

1 Using an electric mixer, cream the butter and sugar in a bowl until light and fluffy. Add the egg white and salt and beat the mixture at a low speed for 5 seconds or until just mixed.

2 Lightly fold the flour and cheese into the mixture. Cover and chill for about 30 minutes.

3 Put 1cm (½ inch) balls of the mixture on to greased baking sheets, leaving a little space between the biscuits. Flatten the mixture with the back of a fork dipped in cold water until the biscuits are very thin. Sprinkle with rosemary.

4 Bake at 200°C (400°F) mark 6 for 6-8 minutes or until the edges are golden. Cool on a wire rack and store in an airtight container.

NOT SUITABLE FOR FREEZING
MAKES ABOUT 20

BACON TWISTS

8 slices lean back bacon

1 Cut each rasher in half crossways, then again lengthways making three or four small strips out of each rasher.

2 Twist each strip into a corkscrew and arrange them in rows on a baking sheet. Put skewers across the ends of the rows to hold the twists in place.

3 Bake at 180°C (350°F) mark 4 for 20-30 minutes or until crisp. Drain well and serve.

NOT SUITABLE FOR FREEZING
MAKES 24-32

MINI COTTAGE LOAVES

500ml (18fl oz) milk
7.5ml (1½ tsp) dried yeast
5ml (1tsp) sugar
700g (1½lb) strong plain white flour
10ml (2tsp) salt
50g (2oz) butter
1 egg, beaten
sesame seeds (optional)

1 Warm the milk until just tepid. Pour into a jug and sprinkle over the yeast and sugar. Stir gently then leave in a warm place until it begins to froth.

2 Meanwhile mix the flour and salt together in a bowl and rub in the butter. Stir the yeast liquid into the flour, mixing to a soft dough – it should be sticky rather than dry.

3 Turn the dough on to a floured work surface and knead well until smooth and elastic. Place in an oiled bowl; cover with oiled cling film and leave in a warm place to rise and double in size – about 1-1½ hours.

4 Knock back the dough, knead lightly and divide into sixteen. Roll three-quarters of each portion into a round and flatten it, then place on greased baking sheets. Top each one with a ball of the remaining dough, pushing the two pieces firmly together with a wooden spoon handle. Cover with oiled cling film and leave in a warm place until doubled in size – about 15-20 minutes.

5 Uncover the loaves, press down to flatten slightly and brush with beaten egg. If wished, sprinkle with sesame seeds.

6 Bake at 200°C (400°F) mark 6 for 15-20 minutes or until well browned and hollow-sounding when tapped. Cool on wire racks then store in a cool place, tightly wrapped.

TO FREEZE:
Pack and freeze.

TO USE:
Thaw wrapped at cool room temperature for 2-3 hours.

These Parmesan and Rosemary Wafers and Bacon Twists make delicious pre-dinner appetisers. The wafers can be made up to two days ahead and stored in an airtight container. The bacon twists are very quick to make and can be prepared a day ahead.

QUICK CHRISTMAS TREE ROLLS

283g (10oz) packet white bread mix
---
milk to glaze
---

1 Make up the bread mix following the manufacturer's instructions.
2 Roll the mixture into small 0.5-1cm (¼-½ inch) balls. Arrange them in Christmas tree shapes on baking sheets, putting four balls in a line for the bottom of the tree, then two lines of three balls, a line of 2 balls and a small ball at the top and a larger one for the trunk. Keep the dough covered while preparing the trees to stop it drying out.
3 Leave to prove as packet instructions. Brush lightly with milk. Bake following packet instructions.

NOT SUITABLE FOR FREEZING
MAKES 8-10

TURBANS OF PRAWN AND TROUT WITH PINK PEPPERCORN SAUCE

Unmould these turbans in time to use the moulds again for the apple moulds in the main course.

225g (8oz) peeled prawns
---
1 egg, beaten

150ml (¼ pint) double cream
---
salt and pepper
---
4 large trout, about 350g (12oz) each
---
butter or margarine

10ml (2tsp) pink peppercorns in brine

250ml (8fl oz) dry white wine

20g (¾oz) plain white flour
---
1 egg yolk

45ml (3tbsp) single cream
---
fresh dill to garnish (optional)
---

1 Purée the prawns in a food processor, adding the beaten egg a little at a time. Chill the mixture for 15 minutes, then gradually beat in the double cream and seasoning. Chill.

2 Cut two fillets from each trout and carefully skin and ease out the small bones. Lightly butter eight dariole or cup moulds, about 100-150ml (4-5fl oz) each, and line them with the trout, skinned side out.
3 Fill the centre of the moulds with the prawn mixture. Cover each mould with buttered foil and stand them side by side in an ovenproof dish, foil uppermost. Pour in hot water to come halfway up the moulds. Bake at 180°C (350°F) mark 4 for 20-25 minutes or until just set. Remove from the oven and leave the moulds to stand for 5 minutes.
4 Meanwhile for the sauce, bring the peppercorns and wine slowly to the boil, take off the heat and leave to infuse for about 20 minutes.
5 Melt 25g (1oz) butter, stir in the flour and cook for a few seconds. Add the strained wine (reserve peppercorns) with any juices from the trout turbans. Bring to the boil, stirring constantly.
6 Beat the egg yolk and single cream together. Add a little of the hot sauce and mix well. Return this mixture to the hot sauce and reheat gently. Add the peppercorns and a little water if necessary to bring to a coating consistency.
7 To serve: unmould the turbans on to individual plates and pour over a little of the sauce. Garnish with dill, if liked. Serve the remainder separately.

TO FREEZE:
Freeze the sauce base only, without the egg yolk and cream.

TO USE:
Thaw at cool room temperature. Reheat the sauce, beat well and complete as directed.

Turbans of Prawn and Trout with Pink Peppercorn Sauce make a sophisticated starter which can be partially made ahead of your dinner party.

ROAST GOOSE STUFFED WITH OLIVES AND PRUNES

225g (8oz) no-soak stoned prunes
350g (12oz) belly pork (fairly lean)
50g (2oz) butter or margarine
50g (2oz) onion, skinned and chopped
12 green olives
salt and pepper
2.5ml (½tsp) dried majoram
2.5ml (½tsp) dried thyme
grated nutmeg
1 egg
75g (3oz) fresh breadcrumbs
5.5-6.8kg (12-15lb) young goose with its giblets
flour
cabbage leaves
parsley sprigs to garnish
thin gravy to serve

1 Soak the prunes for 3-4 hours (this plumps up the no-soak varieties). Drain well, then roughly chop.
2 Chop the pork, discarding the bones and rind. Heat the butter in a pan, add the pork and onion and gently fry for 10-15 minutes. Remove the stones from the olives, chop and add them to the pork. Season and stir in the herbs and a good pinch of nutmeg. Turn the mixture into a bowl and leave to cool. When just warm, stir in the egg, prunes and breadcrumbs. Cool completely.
3 Put the prune stuffing into the tail-end cavity of the goose and if necessary seal the opening with a small skewer. Prick the fleshy parts of the goose with a skewer; sprinkle with seasoning and flour.
4 Roast on a rack inside a roasting tin at 220°C (425°F) mark 7 for 30 minutes. Reduce the oven temperature to 180°C (350°F) mark 4 and cook for about a further 3-3½ hours, pouring off the excess fat as it accumulates during cooking.
5 Drain the goose well and transfer it to a warmed carving dish lined with cabbage leaves. Garnish with parsley sprigs and serve with a thin gravy.

NOT SUITABLE FOR FREEZING

BAKED APPLE MOULDS

6 large dessert apples
50g (2oz) butter or margarine
45ml (3tbsp) lemon juice

1 Peel, quarter and thinly slice the apples. Butter eight 100ml (4fl oz) oval or round metal dariole or aspic moulds and fill with apple slices, pressing down firmly.
2 Dot with the rest of the butter, sprinkle with the lemon juice and about 45ml (3tbsp) water. Bake at 180°C (350°F) mark 4 for 30-40 minutes.
3 Cool and turn out. Serve with the goose.

NOT SUITABLE FOR FREEZING

DIAMOND POTATOES

about 24 medium even-sized oval main crop potatoes
well-seasoned goose or chicken stock
oil

1 Peel the potatoes and make a series of parallel cuts through the top half of each potato, slicing at 1cm (½ inch) intervals but leaving them joined at the base. Make another series of cuts at right angles forming a diamond pattern.
2 Place them side by side in two roasting tins, cut side upwards. Pour stock into the tins to come about a third of the way up the potatoes. Brush the tops with oil.
3 Bake at 180°C (350°F) mark 4 for about 2 hours or until the potatoes have absorbed the stock and are crisp and brown.

NOT SUITABLE FOR FREEZING

Roast Goose with Baked Apple Moulds, Diamond Potatoes, and Julienne of Courgettes.

JULIENNE OF COURGETTES

1.4kg (3lb) courgettes, trimmed
salt and pepper
25g (1oz) butter, melted
grated nutmeg

1 Cut the courgettes into julienne strips.

2 Steam until just tender. Season and arrange in serving dish. Drizzle over hot melted butter and sprinkle with nutmeg.

NOT SUITABLE FOR FREEZING

RASPBERRY CHANTILLY CROWNS

368g (13oz) packet puff pastry
butter or margarine, melted
1 egg, beaten
caster sugar
900g (2lb) raspberries (frozen rather than canned if you cannot find fresh)
icing sugar to taste
300ml (½ pint) whipping cream or Greek-style natural yogurt
2-3 drops pure vanilla essence

Raspberry Chantilly Crown – a cage of puff pastry encloses a pile of raspberries on a pool of raspberry purée. To finish, serve with whipped cream, flavoured with vanilla essence and sugar.

1 Roll out the pastry to a large rectangle and cut into thin strips. Grease two small round metal sieves about 10cm (4 inches) each with melted butter. Place a long pastry strip around the circumference of both upturned sieves, then three to four strips over the outside of the rounded bowls of the sieves to form cages. Press the joins of the pastry firmly together, sealing them with beaten egg.

2 Glaze the pastry with beaten egg and dust with 15-30ml (1-2tbsp) sugar. Bake at 200°C (400°F) mark 6 for about 15 minutes or until the pastry is pale golden. Cool and carefully lift the pastry cages off the sieves. Repeat this process making eight pastry crowns.

3 Thaw the raspberries if using frozen. Purée a quarter of them. Push through a nylon sieve; sweeten if liked with icing sugar. Cover and chill.

4 Whip the cream until just beginning to thicken, then add 5ml (1tsp) caster sugar and the vanilla essence. Whip until the cream holds its shape.

5 To assemble, place a mound of raspberries in the centre of eight serving plates. Top with a spoonful of cream or yogurt or serve it separately. Place the pastry cages over the fruit and pour around the raspberry purée.

TO FREEZE:
Freeze the pastry crowns only in rigid containers.

TO USE:
Thaw at cool room temperature.

BOXING DAY BUFFET FOR EIGHT

The busy cook's dream, this menu, because so much of it can be prepared ahead and frozen. Two golden, savoury mille-feuilles – one filled with ham, cheese and apple, the other with salmon – are the centrepieces, flanked by a colourful Tomato, Red Onion and Olive Salad and a delicious green and white combination of Dutch cabbage and cucumber, spiked up with a sweet and sour dressing. The pudding is a winning combination of sticky, spicy sponge with pears and lemon ice cream. You could, if you prefer not to serve two mille-feuilles, substitute the ham one with the spectacular Gammon with Crunchy Nut Glaze on page 155. This recipe uses a pre-cooked gammon joint so takes literally minutes to prepare.

COUNTDOWN

TWO OR THREE WEEKS AHEAD: Make both mille-feuilles as far as step 5. Freeze as directed. Make the Sticky Upside-Down Pudding and freeze as directed. Make the Quick Lemon Ice Cream.

THE NIGHT BEFORE: Thaw the Sticky Upside-Down Pudding at cool room temperature overnight. If wished, prepare the Crisp and Sour Salad.

ON THE DAY: If necessary make the Crisp and Sour Salad. Cool, cover and refrigerate.

Slice or quarter about 700g (1½lb) tomatoes for the salad. Peel and slice a medium red onion. Place in a shallow dish, mix and cover tightly with cling film. Store in the refrigerator. Make a French dressing. Store at room temperature.

TO SERVE AT 1PM

11AM: Preheat the oven to 200°C (400°F) mark 6. Put *one* mille-feuille in to bake on the top shelf for 30 minutes.

ABOUT 11.45AM: Lower the mille-feuille in the oven and place the second mille-feuille on the top shelf in the oven.

ABOUT 12.15PM: Check and remove the first mille-feuille from the oven, keep warm, loosely covered. Transfer the ice cream to the refrigerator to soften. Toss together the tomatoes and onions, the dressing and a few black olives. Cover and place in the refrigerator.

ABOUT 12.45PM: Test the second mille-feuille with a skewer. Remove from the oven when cooked. Cover loosely with foil and allow to cool slightly.

1PM: Reduce the oven temperature to 190°C (375°F) mark 5, cover the pudding loosely and reheat for 25-30 minutes. Serve the warm mille-feuilles with both the salads.

1.30PM: Remove the pudding from the oven. Allow to stand for about 5 minutes before turning out to serve with Quick Lemon Ice Cream.

BOXING DAY BUFFET FOR 8

Smoked Ham and Cheese Mille-Feuille

Salmon and Prawn Mille-Feuille

Crisp and Sour Salad

Tomato, Red Onion and Olive Salad (see Countdown)

Sticky Upside-Down Pudding

Quick Lemon Ice Cream

SMOKED HAM AND CHEESE MILLE-FEUILLE

Any leftover cooked meat could be minced and used in place of the ham – chicken or turkey, for example.

450g (1lb) frozen puff pastry, thawed
50g (2oz) butter or margarine
225g (8oz) onion, skinned and finely chopped
175g (6oz) eating apple, peeled, cored and grated
1 bay leaf
pinch grated nutmeg
50g (2oz) frozen chopped spinach, thawed
25g (1oz) plain white flour
300ml (½ pint) milk
salt and pepper
175g (6oz) smoked ham, minced
175g (6oz) mature Cheddar or Gruyère cheese, grated
1 egg, beaten
coarse salt
apple slices, fresh herbs or salad leaves to garnish

1 On a lightly floured work surface, roll out half the pastry to a 28×12.5cm (11×5 inch) rectangle. Place on a baking sheet and prick all over with a fork. Bake at 200°C (400°F) mark 6 for about 15-20 minutes or until golden brown and cooked through. Trim the pastry to a neat 25.5×10cm (10×4 inch) rectangle.

2 Melt 25g (1oz) of the butter in a medium sauté pan and stir in the onion, apple, bay leaf and nutmeg. Cook, covered, over a gentle heat for about 15 minutes or until very soft. Remove the bay leaf and cool.

3 Melt the remaining butter in a small saucepan. Stir in the spinach and flour. Cook, stirring for 1-2 minutes then add the milk. Bring to the boil, then simmer until thickened. Season, cover with cling film and cool.

4 Place the cooked pastry base on a flat baking sheet. Spoon on the cold onion mixture to cover, then top with the ham. Spoon the spinach sauce down the centre and sprinkle over all but 25g (1oz) of the grated cheese.

5 Roll out the remaining pastry to a thin rectangle about 33×22cm (13×8½ inches). Place over the pie filling and tuck the raw pastry edges under the cooked pastry base. Brush all over with beaten egg and mark a lattice pattern lightly over the pastry. Sprinkle with salt and the reserved cheese.

6 Bake at 200°C (400°F) mark 6 for about 40 minutes or until the pastry is golden brown and cooked through. Serve warm, garnished with apple slices and fresh herbs or salad leaves.

TO FREEZE:

At the end of step 5, open-freeze the mille-

feuilles, then wrap them.

TO USE:

Unwrap and cook from frozen at 200°C (400°F) mark 6 for about 1 hour or until golden brown and cooked right through. Cover if necessary towards the end of the cooking time.

A Boxing Day buffet for eight – two mille-feuilles of smoked ham and cheese, and salmon and prawn, create the centrepieces of this feast. Most of the dishes can be made in advance.

Salmon and Prawn Mille-Feuille

Ask your fishmonger for salmon tails which are usually slightly cheaper than the middle cuts.

450g (1lb) frozen puff pastry, thawed
450g (1lb) piece salmon
1 bay leaf
4 black peppercorns
125g (4oz) fresh peeled prawns (see Note)
butter or margarine
125g (4oz) onion, skinned and finely chopped
75g (3oz) peeled cucumber, finely chopped
25g (1oz) plain white flour
150ml (¼ pint) milk
75g (3oz) full-fat soft cheese with garlic and parsley
salt and pepper
1 egg, beaten
coarse salt
lemon wedges, fresh herbs or salad leaves to garnish

1 Prepare the puff pastry base by following step 1 of Smoked Ham and Cheese Mille-feuille recipe.

2 Place the salmon in a medium saucepan. Cover with cold water and add the bay leaf and peppercorns. Bring to the boil, cover and simmer for about 15 minutes or until the fish is just cooked. Drain and cool the salmon. Strain and reserve the poaching liquid. Flake the salmon, discarding skin and bone. Cool, then mix the fish with the prawns.

3 Melt 25g (1oz) butter in a medium saucepan. Add the onion and cucumber and fry for 2-3 minutes until golden, then stir in the flour. Cook, stirring, for 1-2 minutes, then add the milk and 50ml (2fl oz) reserved poaching liquid. Bring to the boil, then simmer until thickened. Stir in the soft cheese. Season to taste, cover with cling film and put to one side to cool.

4 Carefully place the cooked pastry base on a flat baking sheet. Spoon on the cold sea-food mixture to cover in an even layer. Spoon the cooled sauce down the centre.

5 Follow steps 5 and 6 of Smoked Ham and Cheese Mille-feuille, sprinkling with salt, but omitting the grated cheese. Serve garnished with lemon wedges, a mixture of fresh herbs or crisp green salad leaves.

TO FREEZE:
Freeze and use as Smoked Ham and Cheese Mille-feuille.

Note: If fresh prawns are unavailable, the mille-feuille can still be made and frozen using frozen prawns, but you must work quickly.

Have the cooked pastry base, the flaked salmon and cold sauce ready and the remaining uncooked pastry rolled out. Assemble the mille-feuille with the still frozen prawns and freeze *immediately*. Cook from frozen as directed in Smoked Ham and Cheese Mille-feuille.

Crisp and Sour Salad

1½ large cucumbers, thinly sliced
225g (8oz) white cabbage, finely shredded
125g (4oz) onion, skinned and finely chopped
salt and pepper
75g (3oz) granulated sugar
300ml (½ pint) white distilled vinegar
2.5ml (½tsp) celery seeds
2.5ml (½tsp) mustard seeds
pinch dried dill weed

1 Mix the cucumber, white cabbage and onion together well in a large bowl.

2 Place all the remaining ingredients in a small saucepan and warm over a gentle heat until the sugar has completely dissolved. Pour over the vegetable mixture. Stir until the salad is well coated. Cover and leave to marinate until cool, about 1 hour.

3 Refrigerate the salad for at least 1 hour or overnight before serving. Adjust the seasoning to taste.

STICKY UPSIDE-DOWN PUDDING

175g (6oz) butter or margarine
275g (10oz) soft light brown sugar
two 415g (14½oz) cans pear halves in natural juices
225g (8oz) plain white flour
5ml (1tsp) bicarbonate of soda
pinch salt
10ml (2tsp) ground ginger
2.5ml (½tsp) grated nutmeg
15ml (1tbsp) ground cinnamon
finely grated rind and juice of 1 large lemon
175g (6oz) black treacle
200ml (7fl oz) milk
2 eggs, beaten
Quick Lemon Ice Cream, natural yogurt or single cream to accompany

1 Warm together 75g (3oz) of the butter and 100g (4oz) sugar. Spoon into a 2.3-2.6 litre (4-4½ pint) shallow ovenproof dish. Drain the pears and arrange cut side down around the base of the dish.

2 Mix the flour, remaining sugar, the bicarbonate of soda, salt and spices together in a large bowl. Add the lemon rind, then make a well in the centre of the dry ingredients.

3 Warm together the treacle and remaining butter. When evenly blended, pour into the well with the milk and 45ml (3tbsp) lemon juice. Add the eggs, then beat well until evenly mixed.

4 Spoon the mixture over the pears. Stand the dish on an edged baking sheet.

5 Bake at 200°C (400°F) mark 6 for about 25 minutes. Reduce the oven temperature to 190°C (375°F) mark 5 and continue to cook for about a further 50 minutes, covering lightly if necessary. The pudding should be firm to the touch and a skewer inserted into the centre should come out clean.

6 Leave the pudding to stand for about 5 minutes. Run a blunt-edged knife around the edge of the pudding. Invert on to an edged platter. Serve warm with Quick Lemon Ice Cream, natural yogurt or single cream.

TO FREEZE:
Cool, pack and freeze.

TO USE:
Thaw overnight at cool room temperature, then reheat loosely covered at 190°C (375°F) mark 5 for 25-30 minutes or until warmed through. Turn out and serve.

QUICK LEMON ICE CREAM

This ice cream appears icy when you first spoon into it, but it is surprisingly smooth to eat.

425g (15oz) carton ready-to-serve custard
300ml (½ pint) double cream
75g (3oz) caster sugar
3 lemons
2 egg whites

1 Place the custard and cream in a large bowl and gently mix together. Add the sugar with the finely grated rind of 2 lemons and 120ml (8tbsp) lemon juice. Whisk until evenly blended.

2 Whisk the egg whites until stiff but not dry. Fold into the custard mixture.

3 Turn into a freezer container, cover and freeze until hard; at least 4 hours, preferably overnight.

4 About ¼ hours before serving, transfer to the refrigerator to allow the ice cream to soften slightly.

NEW YEAR DINNER PARTY FOR SIX

What better way to welcome in the New Year than a beautifully balanced dinner combining the subtlety of Fennel and Orange Soup, the robustness of Beef en Croûte with Horseradish served with a creamy leek and mushroom sauce, and the cool, crunchy delicacy of a Coconut Brûlée served with honey-sweet mango slices? The en croûte element is actually light, crisp filo pastry sandwiched with horseradish, and a far cry from the often cloying richness of beef enclosed in puff pastry. If you are a purist and prefer your beef served naked, the recipe on page 154 could be just right for you: unusual spices add their own subtle flavour to the meat. This spiced beef alternative looks spectacular served as either a whole fillet, accompanied with sautéed broccoli florets and cherry tomatoes, or served cold, thickly sliced and with a salad of blanched broccoli florets, cherry tomatoes and vinaigrette dressing.

Much of the dinner party can be prepared the day before, while the soup freezes beautifully.

COUNTDOWN

THE DAY BEFORE: Make and purée the soup; refrigerate, tightly covered. Prepare the orange rind; cover and refrigerate. Bake the Coconut Brûlée. Cool and refrigerate, but don't grill the top yet. Slice the mangoes, sprinkle with lemon juice and chill.

IN THE MORNING: Brown the fillet of beef; wrap in pastry as directed and brush with butter. Chill until firm, then loosely cover and return to the refrigerator. Mix together the soured cream and the horseradish; cover. Prepare the leeks and mushrooms; chop some parsley; top and tail 450g (1lb) French beans, refrigerate all in polythene bags. Peel and slice the potatoes; leave them soaking in cold water.

TO SERVE AT 8PM

ABOUT 6PM: Sprinkle the Coconut Brûlée with sugar and grill. Return to the refrigerator until required.

7PM: Preheat the oven to 230°C (450°F) mark 8. Dry the potato slices, arrange in the patty tins as directed and bake.

7.30PM: Put the beef in the oven to bake. Cook the leeks and mushrooms; complete the sauce and keep warm, covered. Cook the beans, cover and keep warm. Check the potatoes and beef. Reheat the soup.

8PM: Garnish the soup with fennel and orange and serve.

FENNEL AND ORANGE SOUP

For added richness, stir a little single cream into the soup before serving.

1 large orange
salt and pepper
900g (2lb) Florence fennel
50g (2oz) butter or margarine
15ml (1tbsp) plain white flour
1.4 litres (2½ pints) chicken stock

1 Peel a few strips of rind from the orange. Blanch in boiling salted water for 1 minute. Drain, cool and refrigerate, covered. Grate the remaining rind and squeeze the juice.
2 Thinly slice the fennel, discarding the core and reserving the feathery tops. Melt the butter in a large saucepan. Add the fennel, cover tightly and cook gently until beginning to soften but not brown.
3 Stir in the flour and cook for 1-2 minutes, then add the stock with the remaining grated orange rind and seasoning. Bring to the boil, cover and simmer for 20-30 minutes.
4 Cool the soup a little, then purée in a blender or food processor until quite smooth.
5 Stir in about 90ml (6tbsp) orange juice, then reheat gently. Adjust seasoning and garnish with fennel tops and orange rind.

TO FREEZE:
Pack and freeze.

TO USE:
Thaw overnight at cool room temperature.
Reheat to serve.

NEW YEAR DINNER PARTY FOR 6

Fennel and Orange Soup

Beef en Croûte with Horseradish

Creamed Leeks and Mushrooms

Stick Beans

Sliced Potato Bakes

Coconut Brûlée with Mango Slices

Dinner for six on New Year's Eve – Beef en Croûte, the meat enclosed in flaky, crisp filo pastry, is sandwiched with tangy Horseradish Sauce. Creamed Leeks and Mushrooms make a flavourful accompaniment.

BEEF EN CROÛTE WITH HORSERADISH

The strudel leaves, also known as filo pastry, need no rolling out. Leave wrapped until required as, once opened, the pastry quickly dries up and cracks. The packs can be found in the freezer cabinets of most supermarkets and delicatessens.

1kg (2lb 2oz) piece middle cut of fillet of beef
oil
400g (14oz) packet large strudel leaves, 25·5×51cm (10×20 inches)
50-75g (2-3oz) butter or margarine, melted
horseradish relish
salt and pepper
15ml (1tbsp) sesame seeds
150ml (¼ pint) soured cream
watercress sprigs to garnish

1 Trim the fillet of beef of any excess fat. Seal the meat quickly in a little hot oil in a frying pan. Leave the fillet to cool and drain on absorbent kitchen paper.

2 Use three sheets of strudel leaves; freeze the remainder. Place one large sheet of pastry on a work surface and brush with lightly melted butter. Spread over a little horseradish – about 15ml (1tbsp). Continue layering the ingredients, ending with horse-radish. Reserve some butter for glazing.

3 Top with the fillet of beef and season. Fold over the pastry, sealing the edges well. Trim and pinch the ends together. Place the croûte, seam side down, on a baking sheet and decorate with the pastry trimmings. Brush with remaining butter. Sprinkle with seasame seeds.

4 Bake at 230°C (450°F) mark 8 for about 30 minutes, covering lightly with foil if necessary. (Place on the lower shelf in the oven below the potatoes.) The meat should be medium rare after this time; cook a little longer if wished.

5 Keep warm, uncovered, in a low oven. Slice the fillet and serve with the soured cream blended with horseradish relish and seasoning to taste. Garnish with watercress sprigs.

NOT SUITABLE FOR FREEZING

CREAMED LEEKS AND MUSHROOMS

The sauce is meant to be fairly thin so that it acts as an accompaniment to the beef as well as being a vegetable dish. For a little added luxury, use a few wild mushrooms.

900g (2lb) leeks
225g (8oz) button mushrooms
50g (2oz) butter or margarine
30ml (2tbsp) lemon juice
15ml (1tbsp) plain white flour
300ml (½ pint) stock
30ml (2tbsp) single cream
chopped fresh parsley
salt and pepper

1 Trim the leeks, discarding any coarse green leaves. Split the leeks to open up and then slice into 1cm (½ inch) thick pieces. Wash well and drain. If large, slice the mushrooms.

2 Heat 40g (1½oz) of the butter in a large saucepan. Add the leeks, cover tightly and cook gently until tender but not browned – about 10 minutes.

3 Meanwhile, place the mushrooms in a small saucepan with the remaining butter and the lemon juice. Cover tightly and cook for 3-4 minutes or until the mushrooms are tender.

4 Stir the flour into the leeks, blending until smooth. Mix in the stock and bring to the boil, stirring all the time; cook for 1-2 minutes. Stir in the mushrooms and juices and reheat gently.

3 Take the saucepan off the heat, stir in the cream and a little chopped parsley, then adjust seasoning. Keep warm, covered, in a low oven.

NOT SUITABLE FOR FREEZING

SLICED POTATO BAKES

These are cooked at a high temperature, so keep an eye on them.

450g (1lb) small old potatoes
50g (2oz) butter or margarine
salt and pepper

1 Peel the potatoes, then slice very thinly, preferably in a food processor. Cover the potato slices with cold water and leave to soak for at least 1 hour. Drain the potatoes well and pat dry on absorbent kitchen paper.

2 Melt the butter and spoon a little into twelve patty tins. Divide the potato slices between the tins, seasoning between the layers and ending with a neat layer of potatoes. Spoon the remaining butter over the potatoes.

3 Bake at the top of the oven at 230°C (450°F) mark 8 for 25-30 minutes or until well browned and tender.

4 Ease the potato cakes out of the tins and keep warm uncovered, in a low oven.

NOT SUITABLE FOR FREEZING

COCONUT BRÛLÉE WITH MANGO SLICES

The grill must be really hot before you attempt to caramelise the sugar, otherwise the custard will start to bubble through before the top has browned sufficiently.

100g (3.5oz) packet instant coconut milk powder or creamed coconut
568ml (1 pint) milk
3 whole eggs
3 egg yolks
150ml (¼ pint) single cream
caster sugar
2-3 fresh ripe mangoes
lemon juice

1 Blend the coconut milk powder with 250ml (9fl oz) milk until smooth or dissolve the creamed coconut in warm milk; cool.

2 Whisk the eggs and yolks until evenly blended. Whisk in the coconut milk, the remaining milk, cream and 30ml (2tbsp) sugar.

3 Strain into a shallow flameproof dish so that the custard mixture is 4-5cm (1½-2 inches) deep and comes almost to the top of the dish.

4 Stand the dish in a roasting tin of water. Bake at 170°C (325°F) mark 3 for about 1 hour or until *just* set. Cool, then chill until quite firm – at least 3 hours.

5 Meanwhile, cut the mangoes into neat slices, discarding the skin and stones. Sprinkle the slices with a little lemon juice, cover and refrigerate.

6 Sprinkle the custard with a thin, even layer of caster sugar. Flash under a very hot grill until golden brown. Immediately return to the refrigerator for at least 1 hour before serving. Accompany with the sliced mangoes.

NOT SUITABLE FOR FREEZING

Coconut Brûlée with Mango Slices – to get the topping of caster sugar very crisp and toffee-like, make sure your grill is really hot.

LIGHT SUPPER PARTY FOR SIX

It is nice to buck the seasonal trend and offer something altogether lighter to your guests – and family. In this menu, fish and lots of crisp vegetables make a delicate but delicious alternative to more traditional, meat-based dishes. Nothing has been sacrificed in the way of flavour, and these dishes would definitely appeal to post-Christmas palates. The intense lemony taste of the pudding is mouthwatering, and perfectly complemented by the warm cream sauce – the only rich touch in the whole menu. If even this feels too much, try serving the fresh flavours of the Christmas Fruit Compote on page 90, or even the ultimate Port-Wine Jelly on page 92 – boozy but surprisingly light.

Although none of the dishes here is suitable for freezing, several can be prepared or part-prepared the day before.

COUNTDOWN

THE DAY BEFORE: Make the Light Leek Sauce to the end of step 2. Cool, cover and refrigerate. Prepare the potatoes, cabbage and carrots for the Crisp Vegetable Bake to the end of step 3. Cool, pack in polythene bags and refrigerate. Prepare the spring onion and butter mixture for the Pizzettas, cover and refrigerate. Slice the tomatoes and courgettes. Place on a flat plate, cover and refrigerate. Prepare the cauliflower, if using, and refrigerate.

ON THE DAY: TO SERVE AT 8PM

IN THE MORNING: Cut out pastry rounds for the Pizzettas, cover and refrigerate. Prepare the plaice to the end of step 2, cover and refrigerate. Make the sauce for Glazed Lemon Puddings. Cool, cover and refrigerate.

6PM: Preheat the oven to 180°C (350°F) mark 4. Make the Glazed Lemon Puddings to the end of step 2. Set aside in a cool place.

6.45PM: Prepare the fruits for the Glazed Lemon Puddings, cover and refrigerate.

Raise the oven temperature to 230°C (450°F) mark 8.

7.15PM: Cook the vegetable bake. Cover loosely and keep warm, if necessary.

7.30PM: Complete and bake the batch of Pizzettas.

7.50PM: Cook the Rolled Plaice with Smoked Salmon. Gently reheat the Light Leek Sauce with the cooking liquor. Steam the cauliflower with artichoke hearts, if using, then stir in the black olives just before serving.

8PM: Serve the meal. Gently warm the sauce for the Glazed Lemon Puddings and complete step 4 just before serving.

PIZZETTAS

Look out for frozen, ready-rolled puff pastry sheets in your supermarket. You can also make this recipe using a 375g (13oz) block of puff pastry. Roll it out to 0.5cm (¼ inch) thickness and cut out as directed.

three 20.5cm (8 inch) sheets ready-rolled, frozen puff pastry, thawed

3 spring onions, trimmed and finely chopped

25g (1oz) butter, melted

grated rind and juice of 1 lemon

salt and pepper

30ml (2tbsp) pesto sauce

350g (12oz) medium tomatoes, thinly sliced

225g (8oz) courgettes, thinly sliced

grated Parmesan cheese to serve

1 Cut out six 11cm (4½ inch) rounds of pastry and place on an edged baking sheet. Prick all over with a fork. Bake at 230°C (450°F) mark 8 for about 8 minutes or until lightly risen and golden.
2 Meanwhile, stir the spring onions into the butter, together with the lemon rind and 15ml (1tbsp) lemon juice. Season well.
3 Remove the pastry rounds from the oven. (They may have puffed up quite a bit.) Spread each pastry round with about 5ml

---

(1tsp) pesto sauce. Arrange slices of tomato and courgette overlapping on top of each round and season well. Brush with the melted butter mixture.

4 Return to the oven for 10-12 minutes or until the tomatoes and courgettes have softened and the edges of the pastry are puffed and golden brown. Serve immediately, sprinkled with grated Parmesan.

NOT SUITABLE FOR FREEZING

ROLLED PLAICE WITH SMOKED SALMON

Ask the fishmonger to skin the plaice fillets for you. Smoked salmon trout works just as well as salmon.

6 large plaice fillets, about 125g (4oz) each, skinned
125g (4oz) smoked salmon
juice of 1 lemon
black pepper
100ml (4fl oz) dry white wine
Light Leek Sauce to serve

1 Cut the plaice fillets in half lengthways. Cut the smoked salmon into strips approximately the same size as the plaice.

2 Lay the plaice on a board, skinned side up, and place a strip of salmon on top, patching with more salmon, if this becomes necessary. Squeeze a little lemon juice over each portion and grind over plenty of black pepper. Roll up each fillet carefully.

3 Pour the wine into a flameproof casserole and add the rolls of fish in an even layer, seam side down. (The wine will just cover the base of the casserole.) Cover with a lid or foil.

4 Bring to the boil and leave to simmer for about 10 minutes.

5 Using a slotted spoon, carefully lift the fish rolls on to a warmed serving platter.

6 Carefully strain the cooking liquor into the Light Leek Sauce and spoon a little of the sauce over the fish. Serve the remainder separately.

NOT SUITABLE FOR FREEZING

LIGHT LEEK SAUCE

40g (1½oz) butter
450g (1lb) leeks, cleaned and roughly chopped
1 bunch watercress, rinsed and roughly chopped
60ml (4tbsp) dry vermouth
300ml (½ pint) single cream
450ml (¾ pint) fish stock
salt and pepper

1 Melt the butter in a pan. Add the leeks, cover and cook for 5-6 minutes until they are very soft but not brown. Stir the watercress into the pan. Cook for 3-4 minutes. Cool slightly.

2 Place in a food processor or blender with the vermouth, blend for 1 minute. Add the cream and stock, season and blend again.

3 Place in a saucepan and strain in the reserved liquor. Warm through and serve.

NOT SUITABLE FOR FREEZING

CRISP VEGETABLE BAKE

900g (2lb) potatoes, peeled and chopped
salt and pepper
50g (2oz) butter
450g (1lb) cabbage, finely chopped
450g (1lb) carrots, peeled and roughly grated

1 Cook the potatoes in a pan of boiling, salted water until tender. Drain well and mash, beating in 25g (1oz) of the butter.

2 Cook the cabbage in a pan of boiling, salted water until just tender. Drain well.

3 Stir the cabbage and carrots into the potato. Season to taste.

4 Brush an edged baking sheet with the remaining butter. Spread on the vegetable mixture to a depth of about 1cm (½ inch).

5 Cook at 230°C (450°F) mark 8 for 40-45 minutes or until quite crisp on top. If necessary, brown under a hot grill for a few minutes to crisp further before cutting into squares to serve.

NOT SUITABLE FOR FREEZING

GLAZED LEMON PUDDINGS WITH WARM CREAM SAUCE

Don't be deterred by the long list of ingredients in this recipe: it is very easy to make.

For the puddings
3 eggs
165g (5½oz) caster sugar
65g (2½oz) butter, melted
75g (3oz) flaked almonds
25g (1oz) desiccated coconut
grated rind of 1 lemon
175ml (6fl oz) lemon juice
175ml (6fl oz) milk
50g (2oz) plain white flour
For the sauce
450ml (¾ pint) single cream
grated rind of 2 lemons
50g (2oz) caster sugar
sliced pears, starfruit and grapes to decorate

1 Grease and base-line six 150ml (¼ pint) ramekin dishes.

2 Place all the pudding ingredients in a food processor and blend for 1 minute. Pour into the prepared dishes. Bake at 180°C (350°F) mark 4 for 45 minutes or until a light golden colour and firm to the touch.

3 Meanwhile, place the sauce ingredients in a heavy-based saucepan and bring to the boil. Boil for about 5 minutes or until the sauce has thickened slightly.

4 To serve, turn out the puddings on to individual, heatproof serving plates and add a few pieces of fruit to decorate. Spoon over a little of the sauce. Grill for 2-3 minutes or until lightly glazed. Serve with the remaining sauce.

NOT SUITABLE FOR FREEZING

This Glazed Lemon Pudding with Warm Cream Sauce makes a wonderful, not too rich ending to any dinner party. The lemon flavour is very intense and the fresh fruit adds a good contrast of flavours and textures.

CHRISTMAS TEA FOR SIX TO EIGHT

As this is the season for indulgence, a proper tea with lots of different savoury and sweet things to choose from is sure to be popular, especially with children. The recipes here won't keep you in the kitchen for long on the day, as most can be made in advance and stored or frozen: really, all you have to do is assemble the rolls in the morning, make the Mincemeat and Cointreau Flan filling, and put the rest of your goodies on the tea table. And with any luck, family and guests will be so satiated, you won't have to go near the kitchen to cook until the next day!

COUNTDOWN

UP TO A WEEK BEFORE: Make the flavoured butters and refrigerate. Make the Almond Fudge Cake and the Quick Fruit Cake, the Goosnargh Cakes and the pastry case for the Mincemeat and Cointreau Flan.

THE DAY BEFORE: Mix the mincemeat filling with the bananas. Slice or chop the cucumber and celery, flake the trout or mackerel for the Hot Baked Rolls. Refrigerate. Roughly chop the walnuts. Prepare the orange and lemon rinds. Refrigerate everything separately, covered.

ON THE DAY: TO SERVE AT 4.30PM

IN THE MORNING: If time allows, assemble the rolls now. Refrigerate.

3.30PM: Assemble the rolls if not already made. Add the sliced bananas to the mincemeat, then spoon into the pastry case. Whip the cream with the orange and lemon rind. Add the egg white and complete the flan. Place on a serving plate. Place the Almond Fudge Cake and Goosnargh Cakes on serving plates.

4PM: Preheat the oven to 220°C (425°F) mark 7 and bake the rolls.

4.30PM: Serve the tea.

HOT BAKED ROLLS

Each of the following fillings is sufficient for ten ready-to-bake rolls or two ready-to-bake half baguettes. Allow two to three rolls per person. To make ahead, fill the rolls as directed, place on baking sheets, cover and store in a cool place until required. As alternative fillings, use any turkey or ham leftovers, combined with a little chutney, cranberry relish or mayonnaise.

SMOKED TROUT AND CUCUMBER

25g (1oz) watercress, chopped
50g (2oz) softened butter or margarine
salt and pepper
175g (6oz) cucumber
125g (4oz) smoked trout or smoked mackerel fillet, flaked

1 Blend the watercress with the butter and seasoning. Cut the rolls or baguettes in half horizontally and spread one half with the watercress butter.
2 Thinly slice or roughly chop the cucumber on to the watercress butter. Place the fish on top. Sandwich the halves together and put on a baking sheet. Bake, uncovered, at 220°C (425°F) mark 7 for about 7-8 minutes or according to instructions. Serve immediately.

STILTON, CELERY AND WALNUT

25g (1oz) spring onions, trimmed and finely chopped
125g (4oz) Stilton cheese, crumbled
50g (2oz) softened butter or margarine
salt and pepper
125g (4oz) celery, about 2 sticks
50g (2oz) walnut pieces, roughly chopped

1 Blend the spring onions with the Stilton, butter and seasoning. Cut the rolls or baguettes in half horizontally and spread one half with the savoury butter.
2 Thinly slice the celery on to the savoury butter. Sprinkle the walnuts on top. Sandwich the roll or baguette halves together and put on a baking sheet. Bake and serve as Smoked Trout and Cucumber rolls.

MOZZARELLA, BACON AND ROSEMARY

Gruyère cheese, with its full, rich flavour, is also delicious with this combination.

50g (2oz) softened butter or margarine
15ml (1tbsp) wholegrain mustard
salt and pepper
175g (6oz) mozzarella cheese, thinly sliced
280g (10oz) jar sun-dried tomatoes in oil, drained
175g (6oz) bacon rashers
30-45ml (2-3tbsp) finely chopped fresh rosemary or 10ml (2tsp) dried

1 Mix together the butter, wholegrain mustard and seasoning. Cut the rolls or baguettes in half horizontally and spread one half with the mustard butter.
2 Place the mozzarella on the mustard butter with the sun-dried tomatoes. Grill the bacon and place 1-2 rashers on top. Sprinkle with a little rosemary. Sandwich the roll or baguette halves together and put on a baking sheet. Bake and serve as Smoked Trout and Cucumber rolls.

A tea-time spread to tempt anyone – Hot Baked Rolls with Savoury Fillings to start, followed with Mincemeat and Cointreau Flan, shortbread-like Goosnargh Cakes, Quick Fruit Cake and Almond Fudge Cake.

CREAMY SMOKED SALMON AND DILL

50g (2oz) softened butter or margarine
grated rind of 1 lemon
15-30ml (1-2tbsp) chopped fresh dill or 10ml (2tsp) dried dill weed
salt and pepper
175g (6oz) full-fat soft cheese
30ml (2tbsp) soured cream
175g (6oz) smoked salmon, sliced

1 Mix together the butter, lemon rind, dill and seasoning. Cut the rolls or baguettes in half horizontally and spread one half with the dill butter.

2 Blend the cheese with the soured cream and spread on top of the dill butter. Add 1-2 slices of the smoked salmon. Sandwich the roll or baguette halves together and put on a baking sheet. Bake and serve as Smoked Trout and Cucumber rolls.

MINCEMEAT AND COINTREAU FLAN

For a healthier alternative, use yogurt instead of double cream. Simply fold in the flavourings and the whisked egg white. Use home-made mincemeat (see page 77) or a good bought one.

175g (6oz) plain white flour
75g (3oz) softened butter, cut into small pieces
1 whole egg, separated
2 egg yolks
75g (3oz) caster sugar
2-3 drops vanilla essence
450g (1lb) mincemeat
50g (2oz) ground almonds
30ml (2tbsp) Cointreau
2 lemons
2 oranges
175g (6oz) seedless green grapes, halved
1 medium banana, about 150g (5oz)
300ml (½ pint) double cream or Greek-style natural yogurt

1 To make the pastry, sift the flour on to a clean work surface. Make a large well in the centre, and in it place the butter, the 3 egg yolks, the sugar, vanilla essence and 15ml (1tbsp) water.

2 Using the fingertips of one hand, mix the central ingredients together using a pecking action. When they are well mixed, begin to draw in the flour, using a palette knife to cut through the mixture.

3 With one hand, draw the mixture together and knead gently until smooth. Wrap and chill for 1 hour.

4 Or to make the pastry in a food processor, place the butter, egg yolks, sugar, vanilla essence and 15ml (1tbsp) water in the processor bowl. Work together until just blended, about 4-5 seconds. Scrape the mixture down the sides of the bowl. Sift in the flour and work again in 2-3-second bursts until the mixture resembles breadcrumbs. Empty out the contents on to a lightly floured surface and continue as in step 3.

5 Meanwhile, prepare the filling. Spoon the mincemeat into a bowl and add the ground almonds, Cointreau, grated rind of 1 lemon and 1 orange, the grapes and sliced banana. Mix well.

6 Roll out the pastry on a lightly floured surface to a thickness of about 0.3cm (⅛ inch). Use to line a 19cm (7½ inch) (base measurement) deep, fluted, loose-based flan tin. Bake blind at 190°C (375°F) mark 5 for 10 minutes, then remove the paper and baking beans and cook for a further 5-10 minutes or until the pastry is well dried out. Allow to cool slightly.

7 Not more than 2 hours before serving, spoon the mincemeat filling into the pastry case. Bake at 180°C (350°F) mark 4 for 10-15 minutes until lightly set. Cool. Meanwhile, using a swivel potato peeler, peel the rind from half of the remaining orange and lemon. Blanch and reserve. Finely grate the remaining rind and add to the cream.

8 Just before serving, whip the cream until it just holds its shape. Whisk the egg white until stiff but not dry and carefully fold into the cream or yogurt. Spoon on to the mincemeat and decorate with the reserved rind. This is best served immediately, but you can keep it chilled for up to 1 hour.

GOOSNARGH CAKES

*From Goosnargh in Lancashire, these
thick, rich, shortbread-like cakes were
originally made the size of saucers to use
up the excess winter butter from local
farms. These are more dainty.*

200g (7oz) plain white flour

175g (6oz) butter

50g (2oz) caster sugar, plus extra for
sprinkling

2.5ml (½tsp) caraway seeds (optional)

egg white

1 Place the flour in a medium bowl. Cut in
the butter, then rub it into the flour until the
mixture resembles breadcrumbs.
2 Stir in the sugar and the caraway seeds, if
using. Use your hands to bring the mixture
together and knead gently to a smooth
dough.
3 On a lightly floured work surface, roll out
the dough to a thickness of 0.5-1cm (¼-½
inch). Stamp into rounds using a 6.5cm (2½
inch) fluted cutter. Reroll the trimmings
and stamp out small holly leaves or stars.
Brush the tops of the biscuits lightly with
the egg white and press on the holly-leaf or
star shapes.
4 Place on a lightly greased baking sheet
and dust liberally with caster sugar. Bake at
170°C (325°F) mark 3 for 15-20 minutes. The
biscuits should still be very pale in colour.
Cool on a wire rack. Sprinkle with more caster sugar before serving. Store in an airtight
container for up to one week.

ALMOND FUDGE CAKE

white vegetable fat, for greasing

125g (4oz) whole almonds

125g (4oz) white almond paste

225g (8oz) butter or margarine, softened

175g (6oz) caster sugar

5ml (1tsp) vanilla essence

3 eggs, size 2

225g (8oz) self-raising white flour

5ml (1tsp) ground cinnamon

2.5ml (½tsp) ground cloves

15-30ml (1-2tbsp) milk

125g (4oz) light muscovado sugar

15ml (1tbsp) double cream

1 Grease and base line an 18cm (7 inch)
deep round cake tin.
2 Put the almonds in a heatproof bowl.
Cover with boiling water. Leave for 1-2
minutes, then drain and remove the skins.
Neatly shred the nuts. Grill until golden.
Roll out the almond paste to an 18cm (7
inch) round, cover loosely with cling film.
3 Beat together 175g (6oz) of the butter, the
caster sugar and vanilla essence until pale
and fluffy. Beat the eggs and add a little at a
time to the mixture, beating thoroughly.
4 With a large metal spoon, fold in the flour,
spices and 75g (3oz) of the almonds. Add
enough milk for a dropping consistency.
5 Spoon half of the cake mixture into the tin
and place the round of almond paste on top.
Add the remaining cake mixture and level
the surface. Bake at 180°C (350°F) mark 4 for
1-1¼ hours or until well risen, golden and
firm to the touch. Cool for 5 minutes before
turning out on to a wire rack to cool. Place
on a baking sheet.
6 For the topping, heat the remaining butter, the muscovado sugar and cream until
blended. Bring to the boil, remove from the
heat and stir in the remaining almonds.
Pour over the cake. Allow to cool for 5-10
minutes until set. Store for up to one week.

SPECTACULAR CENTREPIECES

Who can resist a perfectly roasted fillet of beef, or a slice from a golden glazed ham? Just like a whole poached salmon makes an impressive centrepiece for a summer dinner party or buffet, large joints of meat, beautifully cooked and presented, are the perfect focal point for a winter feast. They also usually provide copious quantities of left-overs, saving you from preparing a meal the following day.

At this time of year it pays to order large joints of meat from your butcher in advance. At the same time you could give him any special instructions you might have, such as taking out the bone: in the pre-Christmas rush most butchers are not keen to spend precious minutes performing intricate operations in front of impatient queues.

The beef recipe couldn't be easier and will comfortably serve eight. You could also substitute it for the Beef en Croûte on page 142 if you prefer its simpler presentation.

Whole gammon joints are easily large enough to serve twenty or more people as part of a buffet. Piquant and hot sauces go perfectly with the slightly salty sweetness of the meat, but keep vegetables simple, or stick to salads to avoid overwhelming the flavour of the meat. Mashed potato makes the perfect accompaniment, rather than richer, fried potato dishes.

Spectacular centrepieces – Gammon with Crunchy Nut Glaze, far right, is quick to make and provides a feast for at least eight people.

Home-made Chutneys, Pickles & Preserves

GLEAMING JARS OF CHUTNEYS, pickled fruits, flavoured spirits and vinegars are a traditional part of Christmas. In the days before refrigeration, preserving foods with sugar, vinegar or in oil were ways of ensuring there would be wholesome fruits and vegetables to eat even in the depths of winter. The flavours were darkly rich and pungent, perfect accompaniments to heavy winter dishes.

This still holds true today. The glorious meats and cheeses of the season certainly benefit from being served with a well chosen pickle, while sauces take on an extra depth from a judicious dash of a flavoured vinegar. And left-overs are instantly perked up with a good dollop of chutney on the side.

Heavenly preserves. Pickles, chutneys, and bottled fruits are evocative seasonal flavours. They also make perfect gifts when packed and wrapped with a little extra care and imagination.

159

GIFT WRAPPING CHUTNEYS, PICKLES AND PRESERVES

Preserves of all kinds make excellent gifts, so here are some ideas for packing them attractively. Chutneys, preserved fruits and flavoured oils and vinegars look best in straightforward sturdy preserving jars, or for a more sophisticated effect, in tall, carefully sealed, glass-stoppered jars. Jazz them up with a bow and neatly written label. A pretty touch would be attaching a small draining spoon with preserves such as the Pickled Satsumas and Kumquats. For the Cherries in Brandy, a large glass jar with a chrome handle perfectly complements the rich crimson of the contents. The Conserved Cranberries could be presented in glass jelly moulds, sealed, then overwrapped with cellophane. Decant flavoured oils, vinegars and spirits into old attractive bottles as long as these have good seals. Or seek out old fashioned lemonade bottles with lever stoppers from kitchen shops – perfect for the Lemon and Parsley and Hot Chilli Vinegars.

Cork-topped bottles can be given a bright finishing touch with red sealing wax. Melt enough to give a thick layer and good seal. Scented sugars could be stored in small glass jars with large, flat cork stoppers.

Some of the preserves here do need to be stored in a refrigerator though, so be sure you tell the recipient this. And if you have to travel any distance with them, make sure they are well insulated and cannot warm up. Preserves with a short shelf-life need to be consumed quickly, or they may start to ferment or go mouldy.

STERILISING JARS

Wash the jars first in hot soapy water, or in the dishwasher. Rinse well, then sterilise by placing the dry jars in a fairly hot oven for about 5 minutes. Pour your preserve into them while they are still hot.

SEALING JARS

Use waxed paper discs to cover chutneys, then either a rubber seal or cellophane top held on with an elastic band. Coffee or other jars with screw tops are a better alternative but make sure that acidic chutneys cannot come into contact with metal lids. If you plan to give away some jars as gifts, it is worth buying proper preserving jars (available from most kitchen shops and department stores). They are fairly cheap and, as well as being purpose-made for the job, have an attractive rustic appearance.

RED PEPPER CHUTNEY

This delicious, sour/sweet, hot red chutney goes wonderfully with cold meats and sausages.

1 red chilli
900g (2lb) ripe tomatoes, skinned and roughly chopped
225g (8oz) onion, skinned and roughly chopped
1 red pepper, about 175g (6oz), seeded and finely chopped
300ml (½ pint) distilled malt vinegar
125g (4oz) demerara sugar
5ml (1tsp) salt
5ml (1tsp) paprika pepper
1.25ml (¼tsp) chilli powder

1 Halve, seed and finely chop the chilli. (Wear rubber gloves while chopping to avoid skin irritation.)
2 Place all the ingredients in a large saucepan and bring slowly to the boil. Boil gently, uncovered, until the vegetables are tender and the chutney thick and pulpy, about 1½ hours, stirring occasionally. Pot in sterilised jars and seal with vinegarproof (ie non-metallic) lids. Store in a cool, dry place. Mature for four weeks.

MAKES ABOUT 1.4KG (3LB)

160

CONSERVED CRANBERRIES

An excellent way to serve cranberries with turkey, cold ham or chicken. Or serve well chilled and garnished with lightly whipped cream as a deliciously refreshing, fruity dessert.

900g (2lb) cranberries
450g (1lb) granulated sugar
grated rind and juice of 2 large oranges

1 Pick over the cranberries, discarding any that are bruised or blemished. Wash and dry well.

2 Place in a large bowl with the sugar and orange rind and juice. Stir with your hands until the sugar has completely dissolved and formed a clear liquid surrounding the fruit.

3 Pack carefully in sterilised jars and seal with jam-pot covers. Store in the refrigerator for up to three weeks. Stir well before using.

MAKES ABOUT 1.4KG (3LB)

SWEET AND SOUR CRANBERRY SAUCE

This is delicious with traditional turkey or cold meats and cheese.

2 sticks cinnamon
6 whole allspice
6 cloves
225g (8oz) cooking apples, peeled, cored and chopped
1cm (½ inch) root ginger, peeled and finely chopped, or 5ml (1tsp) ground ginger
450g (1lb) cranberries
300ml (½ pint) cider vinegar
350g (12oz) demerara sugar

1 Tie the cinnamon, allspice and cloves in muslin. Place in a saucepan with the apples, the ginger, cranberries and vinegar. Bring to the boil, cover and simmer for 10 minutes or until the fruits are soft but still retain their shape.

2 Off the heat, stir in the sugar. Return to the heat and simmer gently, uncovered, stirring continuously, for a further 20 minutes. Remove the spices.

3 Pot in sterilised jars and seal with vinegarproof (ie non-metallic) lids. Store in a cool, dry place for up to three months.

MAKES ABOUT 900G (2LB)

PRESERVED WILD MUSHROOMS

1 small onion, skinned and chopped
1 carrot, peeled and chopped
olive oil
2 garlic cloves, skinned
salt and freshly ground pepper
450ml (¾ pint) white wine vinegar
sprigs of rosemary, thyme and parsley
3 fresh bay leaves
6 coriander seeds, crushed
12 whole white peppercorns, crushed
900g (2lb) wild mushrooms, eg chanterelles, ceps, etc.

1 Sauté the onion and carrot in a little oil with the garlic for about 5 minutes or until beginning to soften. Add the salt, pepper, vinegar, herbs, coriander and peppercorns and 450ml (¾ pint) water. Bring to the boil, then boil, uncovered, for 10 minutes.

2 Put the mushrooms in a large, non-metallic bowl and pour over the vinegar mixture. Cover and leave to soak overnight.

3 Strain the mushrooms from the liquid and pack into a jar. Add the bay leaves, herbs and seasoning. Cover with olive oil and seal with a lid. Store for 3-4 weeks before using. Serve with thick slices of warm bread to absorb the mushroom juices.

MAKES ABOUT 2 LITRES (3½ PINTS)

CRANBERRY CHUTNEY

This makes a perfect accompaniment to cold turkey or chicken sandwiches.

700g (1½lb) cranberries
300ml (½ pint) distilled malt vinegar
225g (8oz) sultanas
100g (4oz) seedless raisins
100g (4oz) sugar
15g (½oz) salt
10ml (2tsp) ground allspice
10ml (2tsp) ground cinnamon

1 Put all the ingredients in a large saucepan and simmer gently, stirring occasionally, for about 30 minutes or until the fruit is tender and the mixture is thickened.
2 Pour the chutney into sterilised jars. Seal with vinegarproof (ie non-metallic) lids. Store in a cool, dry place.

MAKES ABOUT 1.4KG (3LB)

PINEAPPLE AND DATE CHUTNEY

Try this with the Swedish Glazed Ham on page 154 or the Gammon with Crunchy Nut Glaze on page 155.

450g (1lb) cooking apples, peeled, cored and chopped
225g (8oz) onions, skinned and chopped
450ml (¾ pint) white wine vinegar
225g (8oz) soft light brown sugar
5ml (1tsp) ground cinnamon
1 medium pineapple, about 1.4kg (3lb)
225g (8oz) fresh dates

1 Place the apples and onions in a medium saucepan with the vinegar, sugar and cinnamon.
2 Heat gently, stirring, until the sugar has dissolved, then bring to the boil. Reduce the heat and simmer, uncovered, for about 20 minutes, stirring occasionally, until the apple has become pulpy and the onions are soft.
3 Meanwhile, peel, core and dice the pineapple, stone and roughly chop the dates. Add both to the pan and boil gently for a further 20-25 minutes, stirring occasionally. The fruits should be just covered in a thick, syrupy liquid.
4 Spoon the chutney into sterilised jars. Seal with vinegarproof (ie non-metallic) lids. Store in a cool, dry place.

MAKES ABOUT 2KG (4½LB)

Pretty floral covers on these jars of preserves turn them into perfect informal gifts. Don't forget to provide the recipient with a label and any storage instructions.

ROSEMARY AND LIME VINEGAR

This is excellent in salad dressings and piquant sauces. Take care when peeling the garlic cloves, as any cuts in the surface will cause the clove to discolour, clouding and spoiling the appearance of the vinegar.

1 litre (1¾ pints) white wine vinegar
large fresh rosemary sprigs
2-3 cloves garlic
1 lime, thinly sliced

1 Place the vinegar in a stainless steel saucepan with a few sprigs of rosemary. Bring slowly to the boil, then boil rapidly for 1 minute. Remove from the heat, cover and leave to infuse overnight.
2 Carefully peel a few cloves of garlic. Place in warm, sterilised bottles. Strain the vinegar into a jug and pour into the bottles. Add a fresh sprig of rosemary and thin slices of lime to each bottle. Seal with vinegarproof (ie non-metallic) lids. Store in a cool, dry place for at least two weeks before using, then for up to six months.

MAKES ABOUT 1 LITRE (1¾ PINTS)

VARIATIONS

HOT CHILLI VINEGAR Omit the rosemary and use about 350g (12oz) small red and green chillies. Boil with the vinegar as before and do not strain. Pour into bottles with the garlic. Seal and store as before.

LEMON AND PARSLEY VINEGAR Boil the vinegar as before with 45ml (3tbsp) chopped fresh parsley and the peeled rind of 2 lemons. Omit the garlic if wished. Pour into the bottles. Seal and store as before.

RED-FRUIT VINEGAR

Packs of frozen soft fruits, such as strawberries, raspberries and currants, are available from most supermarkets.

700g (1½lb) frozen mixed summer fruits
1 litre (1¾ pints) red wine vinegar
30ml (2tbsp) pickling spice
30ml (2tbsp) fresh thyme or 10ml (2tsp) dried

1 Put the frozen fruit in a medium glass bowl and break down roughly with a wooden spoon. Bring the vinegar to the boil with the spice and pour over the fruit. Add the thyme.
2 Cover and leave to infuse for two days, stirring occasionally. Strain the vinegar into a jug and pour into warm, sterilised bottles. Seal with vinegarproof (ie non-metallic) lids. Store in a cool, dry place for at least two weeks before using, then for up to six months.

MAKES ABOUT 1.1 LITRES (2 PINTS)

PICKLED SATSUMAS AND KUMQUATS

900g (2lb) satsumas or other 'easy-peelers'
225g (8oz) kumquats
450g (1lb) caster sugar
600ml (1 pint) white wine vinegar
1 cinnamon stick
5ml (1tsp) whole cloves
5ml (1tsp) split green cardamom pods
5ml (1tsp) coriander seeds
2.5cm (1 inch) piece fresh root ginger, peeled and sliced

1 Carefully remove all the peel and pith from the satsumas. Prick the kumquats with a needle. Place the fruit in a large bowl.

2 Place the sugar, vinegar, spices and fresh ginger into a large saucepan. Bring slowly to the boil, stirring. Simmer for 5 minutes. Pour over the fruit, cover and leave overnight.

3 Strain the syrup into a saucepan. Pack the fruit tightly, with some of the spices and ginger, into sterilised jars. Boil the syrup and bubble to reduce by half. Pour over the fruit. Seal with vinegarproof (ie non-metallic) lids while still hot. Store in a cool, dry place for at least one month before using.

MAKES ABOUT 1.4KG (3LB)

HERB AND GARLIC OIL

Flavoured oils are excellent for marinades, salad dressings, stir-fries and for basting roasts. A split red chilli could also be added to the mixture for extra bite.

2 sprigs fresh rosemary or 10ml (2tsp) dried
2 sprigs fresh tarragon or mint
2 bay leaves
2 cloves garlic, skinned
6 black peppercorns
3 juniper berries
about 1 litre (1¾ pints) olive oil
150ml (¼ pint) walnut oil

1 Place all the ingredients in a sterilised glass jar or bottle with a tight-fitting lid. Seal, then shake well to mix.

2 Store in a cool, dry place for two weeks before using, then for up to three months.

MAKES ABOUT 1.1 LITRES (2 PINTS)

VARIATION

HERB AND SAFFRON OIL Add 2.5ml (½tsp) saffron strands, ground, to the Herb and Garlic Oil.

GOAT'S CHEESES IN HERB AND SAFFRON OIL

Large jars of marinating goat's cheese can be seen on stalls in most French markets and cheese shops. The cheeses are delicious served spread on warm bread with a little of the flavoured oil and browned under a hot grill, and makes an excellent starter or light snack. When the cheese has been used, the remaining oil is wonderful drizzled over crusty bread or mixed salad leaves, or for basting grilled meats and fish.

8 fresh goat's cheeses, such as Crottin, about 50g (2oz) each
1.1 litres (2 pints) Herb and Saffron Oil

1 Place the cheese in a large, wide-necked jar. Gently pour over the Herb and Saffron Oil to cover completely.

2 Seal tightly. Store in the refrigerator for at least one week before using, then for up to one month.

MAKES ABOUT 1.6 LITRES (2¾ PINTS)

RASPBERRIES IN PORT

These would make an ideal present – but remember to make them in advance when raspberries are in season. They are delicious with vanilla ice cream.

700g (1½lb) fresh raspberries
175g (6oz) caster sugar
peeled rind of 1 lemon
600ml (1 pint) port
100ml (4fl oz) brandy

1 Pick over the raspberries and layer with the sugar and lemon rind in sterilised, wide-necked jars.

2 Mix the port and brandy together and pour over the fruit to completely cover.

3 Seal tightly. Store in a cool, dry, dark place for at least one month before using.

MAKES ABOUT 1.4 LITRES (2½ PINTS)

ANISEED GRAPES IN VODKA

Offer the fruit and a tot of flavoured spirit with coffee after dinner.

450g (1lb) seedless black and green grapes
25g (1oz) caster sugar
2.5ml (½tsp) aniseed
450ml (¾ pint) vodka

1 Strip the grapes from their stalks, wash and dry. Prick with a needle and pack into sterilised, wide-necked jars. Heat the sugar gently with 150ml (¼ pint) water until dissolved. Bring to the boil and bubble for 2-3 minutes.
2 Pour over the grapes with the aniseed and vodka. Seal. Store in the refrigerator for at least one week before using, then for up to three months.

MAKES ABOUT 1 LITRE (1¾ PINTS)

CHERRIES IN BRANDY

Fresh cherries soaked in brandy are a real treat. Serve them with cream and a little hot chocolate sauce for a truly indulgent dessert. Or offer with coffee after dinner. The flavoured brandy is, of course, delicious alone.

700g (1½lb) ripe cherries
peeled rind of 1 orange
8 blanched almonds
600ml (1 pint) brandy

1 Wash and stone the fruit. Pack the fruit, orange rind and almonds in sterilised, wide-necked jars.
2 Fill with brandy. Seal tightly. Store in a cool, dry, dark place for at least one month before using.

MAKES ABOUT 1.3 LITRES (2¼ PINTS)

VARIATIONS
APRICOTS AND PRUNES IN BRANDY Soak no-soak dried apricots and stoned prunes overnight in water. Drain, then pack in jars and fill with brandy.
RASPBERRIES IN BRANDY Substitute fresh raspberries in season for the cherries.
GRAPES IN BRANDY Use seedless grapes instead of cherries.

LYCHEES IN KIRSCH

These make a wonderfully light dessert on their own, or you could add a few lychees and some of the syrup to fruit salads.

three 425g (15oz) cans lychees in syrup
200ml (7fl oz) Kirsch
75g (3oz) caster sugar
2 limes, sliced

1 Place the lychee syrup in a medium saucepan and boil down until 300ml (½ pint) remains. Mix in the Kirsch.
2 Layer the lychees, sugar and lime slices in sterilised wide-necked jars. Pour over the syrup; cool.
3 Cover tightly and store in the refrigerator up to one month.

MAKES 1.4 LITRES (2½ PINTS)

VANILLA HONEY

A jar of this would make the perfect small present for any honey-fancier.

½ vanilla pod
1-2 blades mace
1 small jar of clear honey

1 Push the vanilla pod and mace into the honey. Store for one week before using.

MAKES ONE SMALL JAR

VARIATION
GINGER HONEY Stir 1 thinly sliced piece of stem ginger into a small jar of clear honey. Store as above.

HOT CHILLI VODKA

Flavoured spirits are ideal for Christmas cocktails. This one makes an extremely potent Bloody Mary! Remember to strain out the chillies and seeds carefully before drinking the vodka.

1 red chilli
1 green chilli
300ml (½ pint) vodka

1 Split the chillies lengthways. Mix with the vodka in a bottle with a tight-fitting lid.
2 Shake and leave in a cool place for at least two weeks before using. Store for up to three months.

MAKES ABOUT 300ML (½ PINT)

VARIATIONS

CITRUS VODKA This produces a pale lemon-coloured spirit. Try adding a little to sautés of beef or chicken, or stir a couple of spoonfuls into fruit salads or over slices of fresh pineapple. Omit the chillies and add the peeled rind of 3 lemons.
PEPPER VODKA Omit the chillies and add 30ml (2tbsp) lightly crushed green peppercorns. This variation is also delicious served in a Bloody Mary.

REDCURRANT WINE

Try this fruit wine mixed with chilled white wine or champagne for a special Christmas aperitif. Do not discard the strained redcurrants – serve them as a fruity dessert with a little Scented Sugar (see page 168) and single cream. Try the same recipe with blackcurrants or raspberries or a mixture of all three.

700g (1½lb) frozen redcurrants, thawed
1 bottle red wine
450g (1lb) caster sugar
45-60ml (3-4tbsp) brandy

1 Place the redcurrants and wine in a large bowl. Mash the fruit with the back of a wooden spoon.
2 Cover tightly with cling film and leave in a cool place to infuse for three days.

3 Strain the fruit and wine liquid carefully into a large saucepan and stir in the sugar.
4 Heat the liquid and sugar gently, stirring occasionally, until the sugar has dissolved completely.
5 Bring the liquid to the boil, then simmer gently for 10 minutes.
6 Add the brandy and pour into sterilised bottles. Seal.
7 Store in a cool, dark place for at least one week before using, then for up to three months. Shake well before using.

MAKES ABOUT 750ML (1¼ PINTS)

ORANGE GIN

peel of 10 medium oranges
one 75cl (26.4fl oz) bottle of gin
225g (8oz) sugar

1 Cut the peel of each orange into eight sections and place on a baking sheet. Heat in the oven at the lowest setting for several hours until hard and brittle.
2 Place the peel in a wide-necked glass jar and pour in the gin to cover. If necessary, remove some of the peel or add more gin to ensure that the gin covers the peel. Seal the jar and leave in a dark place for six weeks, shaking the jar several times a week.
3 Put the sugar and 300ml (½ pint) water in a pan and heat gently, stirring, until the sugar has dissolved, then bring to the boil and boil for 3 minutes. Remove from the heat and leave until cold.
4 Strain the peel and gin through a nylon sieve, pressing the peel lightly with the back of a wooden spoon. Add the syrup to the orange gin, then strain through muslin.
5 Pour into small bottles and seal. Store in a cool place for two months before serving as a liqueur.

MAKES ABOUT 1.1 LITRES (2 PINTS)

SCENTED SUGARS

These are sugars flavoured with ingredients such as spices, herbs and fruits. They add a unique flavour to all kinds of cakes, biscuits, sweet sauces and hot and cold puddings. These sugars take only moments to make, although you do need to store them for about a fortnight before using them.

VANILLA SUGAR

1 vanilla pod
450g (1lb) caster or granulated sugar

1 Split the pod and bury in the sugar.
2 Store in a clean, dry jar sealed with a lid for at least two weeks before using. Keep topping up the jar with more sugar as you use it.

MAKES ABOUT 450G (1LB)

VARIATIONS
MIXED SPICE SUGAR Substitute 1 cinnamon stick, 2 whole cloves and 1 blade of mace for the vanilla pod.
LAVENDER SUGAR Use 5ml (1tsp) dried lavender heads instead of vanilla pod.
CITRUS SUGAR Omit the vanilla. Dry the peeled rind of 1 lemon and 1 orange in the oven at 100°C (200°F) mark Low for about 40 minutes. Cool and add to the sugar.

Edible gifts are one of the most popular presents you can give at Christmas and people always appreciate something that has been made at home and wrapped with care.

*E*dible Gifts

HANDMADE SWEETS AND CHOCOLATES make ideal presents – almost everybody loves the taste, and the lucky recipient is bound to be impressed by your hard work. Don't let them know how easy it is! All you need is a little time, a steady hand, and top quality ingredients. Do use only the best dessert chocolate, nuts and butter you can find. Remember to use a very gentle heat for melting the chocolate, otherwise it may become granular and lose its gloss which is crucial for giving a professional finish.

Fresh chocolates can be stored in the refrigerator for up to two weeks, or frozen (as long as they are not covered outside in chocolate). For the finishing touch, turn to page 179 for some creative packaging ideas.

Boxes of delights – home-made candies and chocolates are always popular as gifts or to hand around after coffee. Some of these take only a few minutes to prepare.

THE ULTIMATE CHOCOLATE TRUFFLE

Rich, smooth and soaked in Grand Marnier, these truffles are a delectable treat. The key to making them successfully is minimum handling, and always making sure the mixture is firm before touching it. If you rush, and try to roll all the truffles in one batch, you risk the truffle mixture getting too warm and becoming sticky and unmanageable. Always dust your hands with icing sugar before rolling them, and use a gentle but firm technique. When coating the truffles with dry ingredients, such as desiccated coconut, you actually should allow them to become slightly soft so they pick up enough covering. But always briefly freeze the mixture before coating with chocolate. The cake crumbs in this recipe give the mixture firmness so the truffles do not melt the moment they hit room temperature. Chocolate-covered varieties should be kept in the refrigerator until just before serving as the coating quickly softens. If your chocolates have far to travel, do chill them well first, insulate them, then tell the recipient to put them in the refrigerator immediately.

You do not have to use Grand Marnier for these truffles, you could try rum, brandy or Amaretto di Saronno, and shape the mixture into small logs or disc shapes.

For the truffles
200g (7oz) plain dark chocolate or white chocolate
75ml (5tbsp) double cream
25g (1oz) butter, cut into small pieces
45ml (3tbsp) Grand Marnier
25g (1oz) Madeira cake crumbs
25g (1oz) ground almonds
For coating the truffles
about 25g (1oz) flaked almonds
about 25g (1oz) desiccated coconut
cocoa powder
milk chocolate-flavoured strands
icing sugar

125g (4oz) plain dark chocolate
75ml (5tbsp) double cream
about 25g (1oz) plain dark or white chocolate to decorate
edible gold leaf to decorate (optional – see Useful Addresses)

1 To make the truffles, break up the chocolate into squares and place in a medium deep bowl with the cream. Stand the bowl over a pan of simmering water and heat very gently until the chocolate begins to melt. Do not overheat or allow any water to come into contact with it or the chocolate will become granular. Gently stir the chocolate and cream until quite smooth then remove from the heat; leave to cool slightly.

2 Stir the butter into the chocolate until evenly blended. If using dark chocolate, beat the mixture for 1-2 minutes with an electric or hand whisk, until it thickens slightly and lightens in texture (this is not necessary when using white chocolate). Add the Grand Marnier, about 5ml (1tsp) at a time, whisking or beating between each addition.

3 Stir the cake crumbs and ground almonds into the chocolate mixture, stirring until well mixed. Cover the bowl tightly and refrigerate for at least 4 hours – longer if possible – until the mixture is firm enough to handle.

4 Meanwhile for the coating, grill the flaked almonds until golden; cool and roughly chop. Grill the coconut until golden; cool. Place these on separate plates. Sift a little cocoa on to a sheet on nonstick baking parchment. Spoon a few chocolate strands on to another sheet of nonstick baking parchment.

5 Line two baking sheets with nonstick baking parchment. Rub your hands and fingers lightly with icing sugar, then roll small balls of truffle mixture into neat rounds, about 2.5cm (1 inch) diameter. Divide the truffles between the two baking sheets. If the mixture becomes too soft to handle, chill again before completing the rolling.

6 Place one baking sheet of truffles in the freezer for about 30 minutes. Roll the remaining truffles in either the nuts, the coconut, the chocolate strands or the cocoa until evenly coated. Return to the lined baking sheet. The drier ingredients such as the nuts will not immediately stick to the truffles, but if you continue gently rolling them, they will gradually pick up an even coating. Chill the truffles until firm then loosely cover.

7 Meanwhile, break up the remaining plain dark chocolate for coating and place in a small bowl with the cream. (For instructions on covering truffles with white chocolate, see below.) Stand the bowl over a pan of simmering water and heat gently until the chocolate begins to melt. Remove from the heat, stirring gently until smooth. Leave the chocolate to stand until it cools and the mixture thickens slightly.

Place the frozen truffles on a wire rack over a baking sheet. Carefully spoon the chocolate over the truffles or spear with a cocktail stick and quickly dip into the chocolate. Shake off excess, then carefully place on nonstick baking parchment. Make sure the truffles are completely coated in chocolate. Immediately refrigerate to allow the coating to firm up – about 30 minutes.

8 Break up a little of the white or plain dark chocolate for decorating and melt over a pan of simmering water (see step 1). Cool until beginning to thicken, then spoon into a small greaseproof paper piping bag. Pipe the chocolate into swirls over the chocolate-coated truffles. Alternatively, drizzle the chocolate from the end of a teaspoon.

9 Once firm, place in small paper cases, cover loosely and refrigerate. About 20 minutes before serving, remove all but the chocolate-coated truffles from the refrigerator and pile on to a large platter. Leave at cool room temperture to soften slightly just before serving. Decorate the truffles with small pieces of edible gold leaf, if wished, and serve immediately.

TO FREEZE:
All will freeze except those coated with chocolate. Pack in a single layer, overwrap and freeze.

TO USE:
Thaw in the refrigerator for about 3 hours.
MAKES ABOUT 24

WHITE CHOCOLATE COATING

To coat the truffles in white chocolate, allow about 225g (8oz) to coat half quantity of

truffles. Place the pieces of broken chocolate in a bowl over a pan of simmering water. Remove from the heat and allow to melt very slowly, stirring occasionally. Spoon the chocolate over the truffles, re-coating until smooth and shiny. Refrigerate.

USEFUL ADDRESSES
Lakeland Plastics for gold paper sweet cases – 05394-88100
S R Stevenson for edible gold leaf – 071-253-2693

The Ultimate Chocolate Truffles – rich, smooth, and soaked in Grand Marnier these are a deliciously indulgent present. Keep them refrigerated or freeze them, then serve after letting them come to cool room temperature.

ORANGE AND CHOCOLATE LOGS

These little logs also taste delicious dipped in milk chocolate. Try combining the two kinds for a delightful gift.

250g (9oz) soft margarine
50g (2oz) icing sugar
finely grated rind and juice of 1 orange
225g (8oz) plain white flour
75g (3oz) cornflour
75g (3oz) plain chocolate
5ml (1tsp) sunflower oil

1 Cream the margarine and sugar in a bowl until light and fluffy. Beat in the grated orange rind and 30ml (2tbsp) strained orange juice.

2 Add the flours and mix until thoroughly smooth. Spoon the mixture into a piping bag fitted with a 1cm (½inch) star tube.

3 Pipe the mixture on to baking sheets, making about 60 small logs 4–5cm (1½–2inches) in length.

4 Bake at 180°C (350°F) mark 4 for about 15 minutes or until sandy brown and just firm to the touch. Transfer to a wire rack; cool. Store in an airtight container for up to two weeks.

5 Just before packing, melt the chocolate with the oil in a bowl placed over a pan of simmering water. When completely melted, dip in each log to half-coat in chocolate then allow to dry on a wire rack.

6 Pack the logs intended for gifts, interleaved with greaseproof paper.

TO FREEZE:

Cool, pack and freeze at the end of step 4.

TO USE:

Thaw unwrapped at cool room temperature for about 3 hours, then complete as above.
MAKES ABOUT 60 LOGS

WALNUT SNAPS

These wonderfully nutty biscuits are very fragile so if you are wrapping them for presents be extra careful.

50g (2oz) walnut pieces
15g (½oz) angelica
15g (½oz) glacé cherries
50g (2oz) butter
50g (2oz) caster sugar
10ml (2tsp) milk

1 Finely chop the walnuts and angelica. Wash the cherries, dry and roughly chop.

2 Melt the butter in a medium saucepan. Add the sugar, bring to the boil and boil for about 20 seconds only.

3 Remove the saucepan from the heat, add the nuts, angelica, cherries and milk. Beat well with a wooden spoon until the mixture is well combined. Cool for about 5 minutes.

4 Line two baking sheets with nonstick paper. Place spoonfuls of the mixture on them – no more than 5ml (1tsp) each. Allow plenty of room for the mixture to spread.

5 Bake in rotation at 180°C (350°F) mark 4 for about 10 minutes or until well browned. Leave to stand for about 2 minutes, then using a fish slice ease off the paper and place on a wire rack or over a rolling pin to curl as they cool.

6 Cook the remaining mixture similarly, re-using the nonstick paper.

7 Store the walnut snaps in an airtight container interleaved with sheets of greaseproof paper for up to two weeks.

NOT SUITABLE FOR FREEZING
MAKES ABOUT 30 SNAPS

HAZELNUT BISCUITS

For a subtle alternative flavour, replace the hazelnuts with ground almonds.

65g (2½oz) hazelnuts
1 egg white
125g (4oz) caster sugar
15ml (1tbsp) rice flour

1 Brown the nuts under a hot grill. Cool slightly, then rub off their skins and cool completely.

2 Using a food mill or mouli grater, grind the browned nuts.

3 Lightly whisk the egg white then add the ground hazelnuts, sugar and rice flour. Beat well with a wooden spoon until smooth.

4 Line two baking sheets with nonstick paper and place eight spoonfuls of the mixture on each. Spread each spoonful out to about 3.5cm (1½inches) in diameter. Keep them well apart so that they do not run into one large biscuit.

5 Bake at 180°C (350°F) mark 4 for about 15 minutes or until golden brown and just firm to the touch. Cool the biscuits on the sheets for about 10 minutes, then carefully peel off the paper and complete the cooling on a wire rack.

6 Store in an airtight container for up to two weeks.

NOT SUITABLE FOR FREEZING
MAKES 16-20 BISCUITS

GINGER STARS

These are extremely pretty biscuits which can be either hung from the tree or given as a delicious gift.

75g (3oz) golden syrup
100g (4oz) butter
4 green cardamoms
50g (2oz) caster sugar
15ml (1tbsp) ground almonds
225g (8oz) plain white flour
2.5ml (½tsp) bicarbonate of soda
2.5ml (½tsp) ground ginger
1 egg yolk
glacé icing (optional)

1 Warm the syrup and butter in a pan until blended; cool. Split open the cardamom pods and remove the seeds; crush using a pestle and mortar.

2 Place all the dry ingredients in a bowl. Make a well in the centre, add the syrup and butter mixture with the egg yolk. Mix together well to form a smooth dough. Wrap and chill for at least 30 minutes.

3 Knead the dough on a lightly floured surface, then roll out thinly. Using a small star cutter, stamp out the biscuit shapes, rerolling the dough as necessary.

4 Place the biscuits on baking sheets. Bake at 190°C (375°F) mark 5 for about 8 minutes. Using a skewer, immediately make a small hole near the edge of each biscuit. Cool on a wire rack.

5 Store in an airtight container for up to two weeks. Thread ribbon through the skewer holes in the biscuits and hang them on the Christmas tree. Alternatively, drizzle with icing *just* before giving to make an attractive present.

TO FREEZE:
Pack and freeze before icing.

TO USE:
Thaw for about 2 hours at room temperature.
Ice if required.
MAKES ABOUT 30 STARS

Overleaf. From left, clockwise: *Ginger Stars, Hazelnut Biscuits, Walnut Snaps and Orange and Chocolate Logs.*

BITTER ORANGE CHOCOLATES

These are extremely sinful: smooth dark chocolate cases enclosing a creamy, orange filling made from white chocolate, butter, cream and real oranges, topped with almonds.

150g (5oz) plain chocolate
finely grated rind and juice of 1 orange
5ml (1tsp) granulated sugar
225g (8oz) white chocolate
75ml (5tbsp) double cream
25g (1oz) unsalted butter
nibbed almonds and icing sugar to decorate (optional)

1 Break the plain chocolate into a bowl and melt over a pan of simmering water. Brush half the chocolate over the inside of twenty-four small petit-four cases. Chill for 20 minutes until firm. Repeat with the remaining melted chocolate.
2 Heat 45ml (3tbsp) strained orange juice with the sugar until dissolved then bring to the boil. Bubble for 3-4 minutes to reduce to 30ml (2tbsp). Cool.
3 Break the white chocolate into a bowl. Add the cream and heat slowly over simmering water until the chocolate melts. Off the heat, whisk in the orange syrup and orange rind. Gradually beat in the butter. Cool until the mixture is the consistency of whipped cream.
4 Pipe or spoon the mixture into the chocolate cases. Sprinkle with the almonds and dust with icing sugar, if wished. Cover loosely. Store in the refrigerator for up to two weeks.

TO FREEZE:
Pack in a single layer, overwrap and freeze.

TO USE:
Thaw in the refrigerator for about 3 hours.
MAKES ABOUT 24

VARIATION
LIQUEUR CHOCOLATES Replace the orange syrup with 30ml (2tbsp) liqueur, such as Cointreau, Drambuie, etc.

COCONUT CREAMS

A melting combination of butter and coconut sweetened with icing sugar and enriched with condensed milk. The cocoa powder coating creates a delicious bitter contrast.

125g (4oz) butter
125g (4oz) icing sugar, sifted
196g (6.9oz) can condensed milk
225g (8oz) desiccated coconut
50g (2oz) cocoa powder, sifted

1 Cream together the butter and icing sugar in a bowl. Beat in the condensed milk and coconut. Leave, covered, for 30 minutes.
2 Roll into small logs about 2.5cm (1 inch) long. Place on a baking sheet and refrigerate for 30 minutes.
3 Roll the logs in the cocoa to coat completely. Cover lightly. Store in the refrigerator for up to two weeks.

TO FREEZE:
Pack, uncoated, in a single layer, overwrap and freeze.

TO USE:
Thaw in the refrigerator for about 3 hours.
MAKES ABOUT 60

CINNAMON SUGARED NUTS

These are the perfect accompaniment to after dinner coffee, or simply an anytime nibble.

1 egg white
450g (1lb) assorted nuts, such as pecans, walnuts, peanuts
75g (3oz) caster sugar
pinch salt
2.5ml (½tsp) ground cinnamon
pinch grated nutmeg

1 Whisk the egg white with 5ml (1tsp) cold water until frothy. Add the nuts, sugar, salt and spices. Stir well.

2 Spoon the mixture evenly on to one or two well greased, edged baking sheets. Cook at 110°C (225°F) mark ¼ for 1 hour, stirring every 15 minutes. Cool. Store in an airtight container for up to three weeks.

NOT SUITABLE FOR FREEZING
MAKES ABOUT 450G (1LB)

GIFT WRAPPING CHOCOLATES AND COOKIES

The charm of home-made goodies lies in their individuality, so don't try and package them with commercial slickness and precision. Simple materials work best, as they enhance rather than compete with the smooth sheen of chocolates, the rich gleam of home-made preserves. Junk shops, department stores and kitchen shops are good sources of pretty and unusual jars, bottles, baskets and other containers which will outlast their edible contents. For gift wrapping preserves, see page 160.

You can buy special boxes for sweets from various suppliers (see below) but pretty boxes that have held, for example, cards, cosmetics (nothing scented though), jewellery, or other small gifts will do just as well. There are plenty of ideas for decorating boxes in *Decorations to Make & Gift Wrapping*. Display your sweets to best effect in individual sweet cases – brown or black for chocolates or, for glamour, go for gold. Use shredded or crumpled tissue paper under and around fragile sweets. If the box is deep and you have enough chocolates to fill it, cut out card shelves to make layers. Make sure you include storage instructions somewhere in the box where they will be easily found.

Cookies, such as the Spice Cookies on page 24, or a batch of golden mince pies look too attractive to cover up, so you could simply arrange them neatly on a wire tray or inside a pretty wire basket, secure them in place with a tight layer of cling film, then cover the whole arrangement with sparkly cellophane tied with a ribbon bow. Unshelled nuts could be packed into a small twig basket, first lined with a rustic fabric such as cotton ticking or hessian.

You could make your own ribbons for your edible parcels: cut out straight or bias-cut strips of fabrics – madras cotton looks fresh, but any stiffish fabric will do. Use pinking shears for a pretty edge, then iron flat. For a nice, big, fat bow, starch the fabric so it holds the final shape well.

LABELS

Do not forget to add a pretty, informative label that tells the recipient what their gift is, and suggestions for how it should be eaten. Put on any special storage instructions and by what date the contents should be consumed. Make a label from thin card, punch a hole through for the string or ribbon, and tie firmly to your gift. If you think the label looks too plain, edge it with gold pen, or decorate it with a sponged or stencilled-on motif. Or see pages 52-59 for other ideas.

USEFUL ADDRESSES
Squires Kitchen, Squires House, 3 Waverley Lane, Farnham, Surrey GU9 8BB (0252-711749) – supplies sweet boxes, plain or Christmas design, in various shapes and sizes, also sweet cases and moulds.
The Souvenir & Decorations Co, Soudeco House, 1a Aldenham Rd, Watford, Herts, WD1 4AD (0923-817227) – supplies bags, ribbons and sweet boxes.

Easy Meals for After Christmas

AFTER ALL THE RICH food and drink of Christmas, it is a relief to turn to simpler, homelier dishes, which do not take hours of preparation. If the refrigerator is still full of left-overs, don't worry – these too can be incorporated into imaginative meals.

All the following recipes have been chosen for their simplicity and flavour. Most will freeze well. Simple accompaniments such as a crisp salad, baked or mashed potato, or a few seasonal vegetables are all you need for a perfect winter meal.

A welcome return to simpler flavours after the excesses of Christmas – casseroles, soups and tasty dishes made from seasonal foods will taste even better after the richness of heavy dinners and sweet puddings.

CASSEROLES

These are ideal for family suppers or, with a few extra trimmings, as a dinner party centrepiece. Try serving the following with some creamy mashed potatoes, a root vegetable purée, and lots of warm garlic or mustard bread. Or try a rice pilaff with a salad of shredded vegetables on the side.

PORK AND HERB BEAN POT

There are lots of wonderful flavours and textures in this cassoulet-style dish.

275g (10oz) pinto, black-eye or white haricot beans
550g (1¼lb) boned leg of pork
550g (1¼lb) fresh pork streaky rashers
225g (8oz) garlic sausage, in one piece
oil
25g (1oz) butter or margarine
450g (1lb) onions, skinned and sliced
3 sticks celery, sliced
2 cloves garlic, skinned and crushed
30ml (2tbsp) chopped fresh thyme or 10ml (2tsp) dried
30ml (2tbsp) chopped fresh rosemary
30ml (2tbsp) chopped fresh parsley or 10ml (2tsp) dried
400g (14oz) can chopped tomatoes
salt and pepper
700ml (1¼ pints) light stock
4 juniper berries, lightly crushed
175g (6oz) fresh wholemeal breadcrumbs
mixed salad to accompany

1 Soak the beans overnight in plenty of cold water.

2 Trim the boned pork of any excess fat and cut into 4cm (1½ inch) pieces. Cut the rind and any excess fat from the pork streaky rashers, then thickly slice the flesh. Cut the garlic sausage into similar-sized pieces.

3 Heat 15ml (1tbsp) oil and the butter in a 5.1 litre (9 pint) deep flameproof casserole. Sauté the pork pieces and the rashers, about one third at a time, until golden brown. Remove from the casserole with a slotted spoon and drain on absorbent kitchen paper.

4 Lower the heat and add the onions, celery and garlic with a little more oil if necessary. Sauté, stirring continuously, for 3-4 minutes until the vegetables are beginning to soften and colour slightly.

5 Set aside about half of the chopped herbs for the topping. Drain the beans and spoon one third in a layer over the vegetables. Add a layer of pork, rashers and garlic sausage, a layer of the remaining herbs and a layer of chopped tomatoes. Continue until all the beans, pork and garlic sausage, herbs and tomatoes have been used. Season the stock slightly and stir in with the juniper berries; pour over the mixture in the casserole. Bring slowly to the boil. Cover and cook at 170°C (325°F) mark 3 for 2 hours. Remove from the oven.

6 Mix together the breadcrumbs and reserved herbs and sprinkle over the casserole. Leave uncovered and return to the oven at 190°C (375°F) mark 5 for about 30 minutes or until the breadcrumbs are crisp and golden and the meat and beans tender. Accompany with a mixed salad.

NOT SUITABLE FOR FREEZING

SERVES 8

SPICED BEEF WITH HORSERADISH

A glorious rich, spicy casserole with lots of intriguing flavours.

1.1kg (2½lb) stewing beef
oil
450g (1lb) onions, skinned and sliced
1 clove garlic, skinned and crushed
225g (8oz) button mushrooms
25g (1oz) plain white flour
2.5ml (½tsp) ground ginger
5ml (1tsp) medium-hot curry powder
5ml (1tsp) dark muscovado sugar
600ml (1 pint) beef stock
30ml (2tbsp) Worcestershire sauce
salt and pepper
30ml (2tbsp) creamed horseradish
45ml (3tbsp) chopped fresh parsley
Brussels sprouts and mashed potato to accompany

1 Trim the beef of any excess fat and cut into 5cm (2 inch) pieces.
2 Heat 30ml (2tbsp) oil in a 4 litre (7 pint) flameproof casserole. Brown the meat, one third at a time. Drain on absorbent kitchen paper.
3 Lower the heat, add the onions, garlic and mushrooms with a little more oil, if necessary. Sauté, stirring occasionally, for 3-4 minutes. Stir in the flour, spices and sugar and cook, stirring, for a further 1-2 minutes. Add the stock, sauce and seasoning.
4 Return all the meat and bring to the boil. Cover and cook at 170°C (325°F) mark 3 for about 2 hours or until the meat is tender.
5 Stir in the horseradish, adjust seasoning and sprinkle with parsley. Accompany with Brussels sprouts and mashed potato.

TO FREEZE:
Cool, pack and freeze at the end of step 4.

TO USE:
Thaw overnight at cool room temperature, reheat as for Vivid Chicken with Orange and Olives (see overleaf), adding 150ml (¼ pint) stock. Finish as directed in step 5.
SERVES 6

VIVID CHICKEN WITH ORANGE AND OLIVES

The cooking liquor of this casserole is puréed to produce a vibrant, rich pepper sauce. It is a good choice for entertaining, accompanied quite simply with buttered pasta and green beans or salad.

6 chicken breast fillets, about 700-900g (1½-2lb) total weight
175g (6oz) onion, skinned
4 red peppers, about 700g (1½lb)
4 tomatoes, about 275g (10oz)
30ml (2tbsp) olive oil
25g (1oz) butter or margarine
1 clove garlic, skinned and crushed
30ml (2tbsp) brandy
150ml (¼ pint) dry white wine
150ml (¼ pint) chicken stock
1 bay leaf
salt and pepper
2 oranges
6-8 green or black olives, stoned
buttered pasta and fine green beans to accompany

1 Trim the chicken and skin if necessary. Roughly chop the onion, deseed and finely chop two of the red peppers. Skin, halve and seed the tomatoes. Chop finely.

2 Heat the oil and butter in a 4 litre (7 pint) flameproof casserole. Brown the chicken pieces half at a time; remove with a slotted spoon and drain on absorbent kitchen paper.

3 Lower the heat, add the onion and garlic and fry for 2-3 minutes or until beginning to soften but not colour. Stir in the chopped peppers and tomatoes and continue to cook, stirring occasionally, until the mixture gradually begins to soften and becomes pulpy.

4 Return the chicken to the casserole. Heat the brandy in a small pan, set alight with a taper and pour over the chicken. When the flames have subsided, add the wine, stock, bay leaf and seasoning. Bring to the boil, cover and cook at 170°C (325°F) mark 3 for about 45 minutes or until the chicken is tender.

5 Meanwhile, place the remaining two peppers under a hot grill and cook, turning occasionally, until the skins blacken. Peel away the skins with a small knife, running cold water over them at the same time. Cut the flesh into neat strips, discarding the seeds. Holding the oranges over a bowl to catch the juices, use a serrated knife to remove all the peel and pith. Cut down between the membranes to release all the segments. Halve the olives.

6 Remove the chicken from the casserole with a slotted spoon. Purée the tomato and pepper juices, discarding the bay leaf. Return the chicken to the casserole and sieve in the puréed juices. Stir in the pepper strips with the orange segments and any juices remaining in the bowl, and the olives. Simmer gently for 5-10 minutes and adjust seasoning before serving. Accompany with buttered pasta and fine green beans.

TO FREEZE:
Cool, pack and freeze at the end of step 4.

TO USE:
Thaw overnight at cool room temperature. Reheat by bringing it to the boil, then simmering it gently on the hob for about 15 minutes until thoroughly heated through. Finish as directed in steps 5 and 6.
SERVES 6

Opposite page Vivid Chicken with Orange and Olives is a dish full of zestful, tangy flavour. It can be made ahead and frozen. Add a simple salad and buttered pasta for a supper party meal.

GUINEA FOWL WITH GRAPES AND MADEIRA

2 small guinea fowl, about 1.1-1.4kg (2½-3lb) each
15ml (1tbsp) oil
50g (2oz) butter or margarine
2 shallots, skinned and finely chopped
grated rind and juice of 2 oranges
150ml (¼ pint) dry white wine
50ml (2fl oz) Madeira
600ml (1 pint) chicken stock
125g (4oz) toasted walnut halves
salt and pepper
350g (12oz) seedless white grapes
45ml (3tbsp) cornflour
45ml (3tbsp) chopped fresh parsley
roast parsnips to accompany

1 Using sharp scissors, halve, then quarter the guinea fowl (discarding the backbone). Heat the oil and butter in a 5.1 litre (9 pint) flameproof casserole. Brown the guinea fowl half at a time. Drain on absorbent kitchen paper.

2 Lower the heat and add the shallots. Sauté, stirring, until soft. Add the orange rind and juice, about 150ml (¼ pint), the wine, Madeira, stock, walnuts and seasoning.

3 Return the guinea fowl to the casserole and bring to the boil. Cover and cook at 170°C (325°F) mark 3 for 1 hour. Stir in the grapes, cover and cook for a further 30 minutes or until the guinea fowl are tender. Trim the joints; keep warm.

4 Blend the cornflour to a smooth paste with a little water. Add to the casserole and bring to the boil, stirring, until the juices are lightly thickened. Stir in the parsley; season to taste.

TO FREEZE:
Cook for 1 hour only at step 3, without the grapes.

TO USE:
Thaw overnight at cool room temperature. Add the grapes and reheat as for Vivid Chicken with Orange and Olives. Finish as directed in step 4.
SERVES 6

CREAMY SMOKED HADDOCK CASSEROLE

A welcome relief from meat, this succulent, warming fish dish has lots of tasty sauce so is best served in soup bowls with plenty of crusty white bread.

450g (1lb) fresh haddock fillet
225g (8oz) smoked haddock fillet
25g (1oz) butter or margarine
350g (12oz) onion, skinned and sliced
175g (6oz) courgettes, thickly sliced
175g (6oz) carrots, peeled and thickly sliced
600ml (1 pint) light stock
350g (12oz) old potatoes, peeled and cut into large chunks
125g (4oz) cooked peeled prawns
15ml (1tbsp) cornflour
150ml (¼ pint) single cream
30-45ml (2-3tbsp) chopped fresh parsley
salt and pepper
crusty white bread to accompany

1 Skin the haddock and cut the flesh into large pieces.

2 Melt the butter in a 4 litre (7 pint) flameproof casserole. Add the onion, courgettes and carrots and sauté gently, stirring, for 3-4 minutes.

3 Add the stock and potatoes and bring to the boil. Cover and simmer gently on the hob or in the oven at 170°C (325°F) mark 3 for 30 minutes or until all the vegetables are tender.

4 Add the haddock and prawns; bring back to the boil. Cover and simmer on the hob or return to the oven for a further 5 minutes until the fish is cooked.

5 Mix the cornflour to a smooth paste with a little water. Stir into the casserole and bring to the boil; bubble for 1 minute, stirring all the time.

6 Just before serving, stir in the cream and parsley. Warm gently and adjust seasoning. Accompany with plenty of crusty white bread.

NOT SUITABLE FOR FREEZING
SERVES 6

Opposite *Guinea Fowl with Grapes and Madeira sounds sophisticated but is very easy to make, as all the ingredients are added to just one pot.*

VEGETARIAN DISHES

Whether you never eat meat, or simply crave a change after an orgy of Christmas turkey eating, the following recipes should appeal. Based on seasonal vegetables, they offer intriguing and unexpected combinations of flavours which make them more than able to stand comparison with meat-based dishes. Some of them take literally minutes to prepare, like the Winter Salad – a wonderful zingy mixture of tastes, colours and textures. Combine with a warming dish such as Sliced Baked Vegetables or Mixed Lentil Casserole and you have the perfect winter supper.

MIXED LENTIL CASSEROLE

350g (12oz) mooli (white radish)
450g (1lb) button mushrooms
25g (1oz) fresh root ginger
5ml (1tsp) cumin seeds
15ml (1tbsp) coriander seeds
5ml (1tsp) mustard seeds
45ml (3tbsp) olive oil
350g (12oz) onions, skinned and sliced
450g (1lb) carrots, peeled and sliced
350g (12oz) trimmed leeks, sliced
2 cloves garlic, skinned and crushed
1.25ml (¼tsp) ground turmeric
175g (6oz) split red lentils
50g (2oz) brown/green lentils
salt and pepper
60ml (4tbsp) chopped fresh coriander

1 Peel the mooli and roughly chop. Halve any large mushrooms. Peel and grate or finely chop the ginger. Crush the cumin, coriander and mustard seeds in a mortar with a pestle or in a strong bowl with the end of a rolling pin.

2 Heat the oil in a 5.1 litre (9 pint) flame-proof casserole. Add the onions, carrots, leeks and mooli and sauté, stirring, for 2-3 minutes, then add the mushrooms, garlic, ginger, turmeric and crushed spices. Sauté for a further 2-3 minutes.

3 Rinse and drain the lentils. Stir into the casserole with 750ml (1¼ pints) boiling water. Season and return to the boil. Cover and cook at 180°C (350°F) mark 4 for about 45 minutes or until the vegetables and lentils are tender. Stir in the fresh coriander and adjust seasoning before serving.

NOT SUITABLE FOR FREEZING
SERVES 6

SLICED BAKED VEGETABLES

25g (1oz) butter or margarine
225g (8oz) onions, skinned and thinly sliced
450g (1lb) carrots, peeled and thinly sliced
225g (8oz) turnips, peeled and thinly sliced
225g (8oz) parsnips, peeled and thinly sliced
1 large clove garlic, skinned and crushed
45ml (3tbsp) chopped parsley
salt and pepper
450ml (¾ pint) stock
15ml (1tbsp) coarse-grain mustard
75g (3oz) Cheddar cheese, grated

1 Heat the butter in a shallow flameproof dish. Add the onions and fry until browned.
2 Stir in the remaining vegetables with the garlic, parsley and seasoning. Mix together the stock and mustard and pour over the vegetables.
3 Cover tightly and bake at 180°C (350°F) mark 4 for about 1¼ hours or until the vegetables are just tender.
4 Sprinkle over the cheese. Increase the oven temperature to 220°C (425°F) mark 7 and bake for a further 25-30 minutes.

NOT SUITABLE FOR FREEZING
SERVES 6

Winter Salad

1 lemon
30ml (2tbsp) olive oil
150ml (¼ pint) natural yogurt
salt and pepper
2 apples
225g (8oz) red cabbage, finely sliced
1 small onion, skinned and thinly sliced
4 sticks celery, thinly sliced
125g (4oz) Cheddar cheese, cubed
50g (2oz) unsalted peanuts in skins
celery leaves to garnish (optional)

1 In a large bowl whisk together the grated rind of ½ lemon, 45ml (3tbsp) lemon juice, the olive oil and yogurt. Season well.
2 Quarter, core and roughly chop the apples. Toss in the dressing.
3 Toss the cabbage, onion, celery and cheese with the apples, mixing well. Sprinkle with peanuts and garnish with celery leaves.

NOT SUITABLE FOR FREEZING
SERVES 4

Curried potato and cauliflower casserole

Remember to stir the juices while the casserole is simmering; potatoes readily stick to the cooking dish if given a chance.

700g (1½lb) old potatoes
225g (8oz) cauliflower florets – 1 small cauliflower
oil
225g (8oz) onions, skinned and roughly chopped
15ml (1tbsp) mild curry powder
50g (2oz) creamed coconut
400g (14oz) can chopped tomatoes
15ml (1tbsp) lemon juice
salt and pepper
45ml (3tbsp) chopped fresh coriander

1 Peel the potatoes, then cut into bite-sized

pieces. Divide the cauliflower into similar-sized pieces.
2 Heat a little oil in a medium flameproof casserole. Add the potatoes, onion, cauliflower and curry powder and fry gently for 2-3 minutes, stirring frequently.
3 Meanwhile, chop the coconut and blend until smooth with 450ml (15fl oz) hot water. Stir into the casserole with the tomatoes, lemon and seasoning. Bring to the boil.
4 Cover the casserole and simmer for 20-25 minutes or until the vegetables are quite tender, stirring occasionally to prevent sticking.
5 Stir in the coriander and adjust seasoning.

NOT SUITABLE FOR FREEZING
SERVES 6

Sautéed Aubergines and Courgettes

Choose small aubergines, in preference to the larger variety, as they are less bitter.

4 small aubergines
salt and freshly ground pepper
450g (1lb) courgettes
45ml (3tbsp) olive oil
30ml (2tbsp) chopped fresh oregano or marjoram
15ml (1tbsp) toasted sesame seeds

1 Cut the aubergines lengthways into 2.5cm (1 inch) slices. Cut the slices across into 1cm (½ inch) wide fingers. Put the aubergines in a colander and sprinkle generously with salt. Leave for at least 30 minutes.
2 Rinse the aubergines and dry thoroughly. Trim the courgettes and cut into pieces about the same size as the aubergine.
3 Heat the oil in a large heavy-based frying pan and sauté the aubergines for 3 minutes. Add the courgettes and continue cooking for 3-4 minutes or until just tender but not soggy. Season with salt and pepper. Serve garnished with oregano or marjoram and sprinkle with the sesame seeds.

NOT SUITABLE FOR FREEZING
SERVES 8

AND NOW FOR THE LEFT-OVERS . . .

The following recipes and suggestions should take care of most post-Christmas remnants. Several of the dishes involve adding pastry, pasta, potatoes or some other filling ingredient to help make the meat go further – a thrifty idea for whenever you feel uncertain you have enough to satisfy the family's appetites.

Food Safety

Leftovers are a potential source of food poisoning so take care to watch the following points:

● Cool leftovers rapidly, then store, wrapped, in the refrigerator well away from other foods.

● Never use leftovers in a dish you cook then freeze and reheat. It could become a source of harmful bacteria.

● Don't keep leftovers for more than 48 hours before consuming, and make sure they are *thoroughly* reheated if you are serving them hot. If you have added a sauce for example and chunks of meat are being heated in it, take out a piece of meat to test it is *hot* at the centre.

● If in doubt about any leftovers, don't risk it – throw them out, well wrapped to keep them from being consumed by pets.

TURKEY TERRINE

225g (8oz) cooked turkey meat
225g (8oz) turkey or pig's liver
175g (6oz) thin streaky bacon rashers, rinded
1 medium onion, skinned
1 clove garlic, skinned and crushed
225g (8oz) sausagemeat
15ml (1tbsp) chopped fresh sage or 5ml (1tsp) dried
45ml (3tbsp) double cream
30ml (2tbsp) brandy
1 egg
salt and pepper
1 bay leaf

1 Mince the turkey, liver, 50g (2oz) of the bacon and the onion (or blend in a food processor).

2 Put the mixture in a bowl. Add the garlic and rest of the ingredients, except the bay leaf and remaining bacon. Mix well.

3 Stretch the remaining bacon rashers with the flat side of the blade of a cook's knife. Use the bacon rashers to line a 1.1 litre (2 pint) terrine or loaf tin.

4 Spoon the meat mixture into the tin and place the bay leaf on top. Cover the terrine tightly with foil, then stand the container in a roasting tin.

5 Pour 4cm (1½ inches) hot water into the roasting tin. Bake at 170°C (325°F) mark 3 for 1½ hours or until firm. Remove from the roasting tin. Cool for 2 hours. Put heavy weights on top of the terrine over the foil. Chill overnight in the refrigerator.

6 To serve, remove foil, turn the terrine on to a plate and cut into even slices.

TO FREEZE:

Pack and freeze.

TO USE:

Thaw overnight at cool room temperature.
SERVES 8

STILTON AND BROCCOLI SOUP

25g (1oz) butter or margarine
175g (6oz) onion, skinned and sliced
175g (6oz) broccoli, sliced
45ml (3tbsp) red lentils
1 large bunch watercress, rinsed and roughly chopped
900ml (1½ pints) chicken stock
50-125g (2-4oz) Stilton or to taste, crumbled
salt and pepper
chopped parsley to garnish

1 Heat the butter in a saucepan. Add the onion and broccoli and fry until soft.

2 Stir in the lentils, watercress and stock. Bring to the boil, cover and simmer for about 20 minutes.

3 Purée the soup in a food processor or blender until smooth. Reheat. Add the Stilton. Adjust the seasoning to taste. Serve garnished with parsley.

NOT SUITABLE FOR FREEZING
SERVES 4

PASTA PILLOWS

Cooked, flaked fish or finely chopped leftover ham could be used here. The pasta must be fresh, pliable and not cracked. Dried pasta won't stick together for the pillows.

90g (3½oz) butter or margarine
2.5cm (1 inch) piece fresh root ginger, peeled and finely chopped
125g (4oz) onion, skinned and finely chopped
2.5ml (½tsp) paprika pepper
75g (3oz) plain white flour
225g (8oz) low-fat soft cheese
15ml (1tbsp) lemon juice
225g (8oz) fresh uncooked peeled prawns, finely chopped
salt and pepper
350g (12oz) fresh egg pasta lasagne
oil
2 eggs
100g (4oz) frozen spinach, thawed
1 clove garlic, skinned and crushed
900ml (1½ pints) skimmed milk

1 Melt 40g (1½oz) of the butter in a medium saucepan and sauté the ginger and onion with the paprika for 3-4 minutes until golden. Stir in 15g (½oz) of the flour. Cook, stirring, for 1 minute, then add the cheese and lemon juice. Cook for a further 1 minute. Off the heat, stir in the prawns and seasoning. Cool.

2 Cook the pasta in boiling salted water with added oil until just tender. Drain, rinse with warm water, then spread out on absorbent kitchen paper to dry for 5 minutes only. Brush one side of the lasagne sheets with one beaten egg. Place a heaped spoonful of the prawn mixture in the centre of the bottom half of each sheet. Spread out a little to within 0.5cm (¼ inch) of the edges. Fold the lasagne over to enclose. Press the edges together firmly to seal. Cover.

3 Meanwhile, squeeze all the excess moisture from the spinach and finely chop. Melt the remaining butter in a saucepan and sauté the spinach with the garlic for 1-2 minutes. Stir in the remaining flour and the milk. Bring to the boil. Cook, stirring, for 1-2 minutes until thickened; season. Off the

heat, beat in the remaining egg yolk.

4 Whisk the egg white until stiff but not dry and fold into the spinach sauce. Spoon 300ml (½ pint) sauce in the base of a large greased 3.4 litre (6 pint) ovenproof dish. Place the pasta pillows in a slightly overlapping layer on top. Pour over the remaining sauce.

5 Bake at 180°C (350°F) mark 4 for 35-45 minutes or until golden brown.

TO FREEZE:

Place the pasta pillows (without sauce) on baking sheets; cover and open freeze. Pack when firm.

TO USE:

Spread the frozen pillows on lined baking sheets, cover and thaw overnight at cool room temperature. Make the sauce and complete the recipe above.

SERVES 4

Soups taste better made with real stock, and the turkey carcass makes an ideal base for stock. Once made, add pieces of cooked ham or turkey for extra flavour and add a dash of lemon juice or cream to finish.

GOLDEN CHICKEN AND WATERCRESS BAKE

Try using only one chicken and mixing it with 450g (1lb) left-over cooked ham or gammon, shredded.

two 1.4kg (3lb) chickens
salt and pepper
sliced vegetables for flavouring stock
2 bunches watercress, rinsed and finely chopped
1.1kg (2½lb) old potatoes, peeled
50g (2oz) butter or margarine
50g (2oz) plain white flour
paprika pepper
300ml (½ pint) milk
300ml (½ pint) single cream
125g (4oz) strong Cheddar or Lancashire cheese, grated

1 Place the chicken in large pans of salted water with slices of vegetables to flavour. Bring to the boil, cover and simmer for about 50 minutes or until the chickens are cooked through. Cool in the liquid for about 30 minutes.
2 Lift out the chickens, reserving the stock. Cut the flesh into bite-sized pieces, discarding skin and bone. Place in a large, shallow ovenproof dish. Mix the watercress with the chicken, cover and refrigerate. Boil down the cooking liquid until well reduced. Strain and set aside. Skim off any fat.
3 Meanwhile, cut the potatoes into large pieces. Boil in salted water for 5 minutes only. Drain; cut into 2.5cm (1 inch) pieces.
4 Melt the butter in a large saucepan. Add the flour with 5ml (1tsp) paprika and cook, stirring, for 1 minute. Mix in the milk with 450ml (¾ pint) reserved stock (freeze any remaining stock). Season and bring to the boil, stirring all the time. Simmer for 3-4 minutes. Take off the heat and stir in the cream and cheese. Adjust seasoning. Pour over the chicken and watercress. Top with par-boiled potatoes.
5 Bake uncovered at 200°C (400°F) mark 6 for about 1 hour or until the potatoes are cooked and golden brown. Sprinkle with more paprika to serve.

TO FREEZE:
Cool, pack and freeze at the end of step 4.

TO USE:
Thaw overnight at cool room temperature. Bake as before.
SERVES 8

TIPSY CHRISTMAS TRIFLE

This is a delicious way of using up left-over fruit salad, sponge cake (use trifle sponges instead if you prefer) and Christmas pudding. It is very rich, so a little goes a long way.

4 trifle sponges or 75g (3oz) sponge cake
30ml (2tbsp) brandy
10ml (2tsp) powdered gelatine
300ml (½ pint) pouring custard
225g (8oz) leftover fruit salad
150ml (¼ pint) double cream or 150ml (¼ pint) soured cream
at least 175g (6oz) leftover Christmas pudding
whipped cream to decorate (optional)
1 orange

1 Crumble the trifle sponges into a deep serving bowl. Spoon over the brandy.
2 Soak the gelatine in 30ml (2tbsp) water in a bowl, then place over a pan of hot water and stir to dissolve. Stir into the custard. Cool.
3 Spoon the fruit salad, with 60ml (4tbsp) of its juice, over the cake mixture. Slowly pour in the custard. Chill the mixture in the refrigerator until set.
4 Lightly whip the double cream, if using, and spread evenly over the trifle.
5 Crumble the Christmas pudding on to a baking sheet. Grill for 3-4 minutes only. Allow to cool.
6 Sprinkle the pudding crumbs over the trifle to cover. Decorate with whipped cream, grated orange rind and a few orange segments. Chill until required.

NOT SUITABLE FOR FREEZING
SERVES 6-8

BAKED SATSUMA CUSTARD

6 satsumas, 450g (1lb) total weight
300ml (½ pint) water
25g (1oz) sugar
50g (2oz) caster sugar
568ml (1 pint) milk
4 eggs
30ml (2tbsp) Grand Marnier

1 Peel the rind of one of the satsumas. Bring it slowly to the boil in a pan with the water and the 25g (1oz) sugar. Simmer for 3-4 minutes. Strain and reserve the syrup.

2 Peel the remaining fruit and place the peel in a food processor with the caster sugar, milk and eggs. Blend.

3 Strain into six 150ml (¼ pint) ovenproof dishes. Place them in a roasting tin half full of water. Bake at 170°C (325°F) mark 3 for about 1 hour until lightly set. Cool and chill.

4 Segment the peeled fruit and place in the syrup with the Grand Marnier. Set aside until required.

5 To serve, decorate the cooled custards with a few satsuma segments and serve the syrup separately.

NOT SUITABLE FOR FREEZING
SERVES 6

MORE IDEAS FOR LEFT-OVERS

● Jars of cranberry sauce rarely get finished. Don't waste this piquant relish: serve it with all kinds of cold meats or stir a little into chicken gravy for a hint of fruitiness. Top slices of goat's cheese with a spoonful and bake on a disc of puff pastry. This makes a delicious starter.

● Bread sauce need not be thrown away either. Mix with a little finely chopped ham, add some chopped spring onions, melted butter or leftover whipped cream. Serve over hot jacket potatoes or fold spoonfuls of it into mashed potato.

● Mincemeat can be put into tubs and frozen. Use with sliced apples in pies or as a delicious filling for baked apples.

● Pieces of cheese often get left in the refrigerator and forgotten about. Use any hard blue cheese, particularly Stilton, in the tasty Stilton and Broccoli Soup recipe on page 190.

● Add whole, or broken, left-over nuts to muesli.

● Dates can be stoned and chopped coarsely, then added to your favourite flapjack recipe. Chopped dates store well in jars and can be frozen in polythene bags and thawed at room temperature. If they become too sticky, run a little boiling water over them. Fresh dates are also wonderful in fruit salads.

● Smoked salmon freezes well as long as the slices are interleaved with foil, wax paper or cling film. Serve it for brunch with scrambled eggs and hot brown muffins, or as a starter with lemon and black pepper, or folded round cream cheese and prawns.

● Weed out fruits past their best, then arrange the rest prettily on a platter. People are far more likely to be tempted to eat them up.

● Turkey and ham chopped into a creamy sauce makes a delicious savoury filling for pancakes and jacket potatoes. Or try layering the mixture between layers of cooked lasagne, topping it with béchamel sauce and grated cheese and baking in the oven as for ordinary lasagne.

● Make a tasty soup with puréed cooked sprouts, turkey stock and a dash of cream to serve. Add lemon juice and chopped herb for extra piquancy.

● Don't forget that the turkey carcass makes excellent stock for soups and stews. Chop up the carcass so it fits into a large pan, then cover it with cold water. Add vegetables, a bouquet garni and seasoning. Bring to the boil, removing any scum, then simmer for about 2 hours, topping up with water to keep the carcass covered. Add bits of cooked ham or turkey meat to the final recipe, if you are making soup from the turkey stock.

Suppliers

All the following firms can supply by mail order and recommend early ordering for Christmas.

FISH AND SHELLFISH

CAREW OYSTERS
Tything Barn, West Williamston, Carew, Kilgetty, Dyfed SA68 OTN Wales
Tel 0646 651452
Shellfish farmers who grow, grade, purify and pack their own Pacific oysters. Brochure on request. Gift service. Minimum order.

CRANNOG SEAFOODS LTD
Blar Mhor, Fort William, Invernesshire PH33 7NG
Fresh and smoked langoustine, smoked fish. Gift service available.

HEAD MILL TROUT FARM LTD
Head Mill, Umberleigh, Devon EX37 9HA
Tel 0769 80863
Smoked and fresh trout, filleted, potted and pâté products.

HEBRIDES HARVEST LTD
Isle of Harris PA85 3BG Scotland
Tel 0859 2323
Fax 0859 2373
Smoked and fresh farmed salmon.

INVERNAIRN SALMON & GAME CO LTD
Unit 16, Balmakeith Ind Estate, Nairn Highland IV12 5QW Scotland
Tel 0667 54737
Fax 0667 52250
Smoked, fresh and pâtéd Scottish salmon. Also gravadlax.

LANG-GEO OYSTERS
Finstown, Orkney KW17 2EL Scotland
Tel 0856 76544
Fax 0856 76544
Oysters, scallops, mussels and other shellfish grown and packed on site.

LOCH FYNE OYSTERS
Clachan Farm, Cairndow, Argyll PA26 8BH Scotland
Tel 04996 264
Fax 04996 234
Fresh and smoked shellfish and fish, also pigeon breasts, cods' roe and fresh and smoked game. Mixed packs for hampers can be supplied.

MULL SHELLFISH LTD
Dunan, Artun, Bunessan, Isle of Mull PA67 6DH Scotland
Tel 06817 295
Smoked mussels, salmon, salmon pâté and gravadlax.

MURRAY OF CROMARTY
The Smokehouse, Alness, Ross-shire IV17 OXS Scotland
Tel 0349 882152
Fax 0349 882176
Fresh and smoked salmon, also barbecued salmon portions.

SEASALTER SHELLFISH (WHITSTABLE) LTD
The Harbour, Whitstable, Kent CT5 1AB
Tel 0227 272003
Fax 0227 264829
Gigas oysters supplied by the dozen or in tubs. Also Manila clams. Leaflets on request. Minimum order.

MEAT, POULTRY AND GAME

FLETCHERS FINE FOODS
Reediehill, Auchtermuchty, Fife, KY14 7HS Scotland
Tel 0337 28369
Fax 0337 27001
Venison steaks, haggis, sausages, burgers, also smoked venison. Brochures and recipes on request.

GB GEESE
Lings View Farm, 10 Middle St, Croxton Kerrial, Grantham, Lincs NG23 1QP
Tel 0476 870394
Fresh free range geese, long legged or oven ready, available from late September to December. Also smoked goose breast fillets, boned geese and goose legs available all year round. Geese can be boned and filled for special occasions. Free range Bronze turkeys supplied for Christmas.

GOODMAN'S GEESE
Walsgrove Farm, Gt Witley, Worcester WR6 6JJ
Tel 0299 896272
Free range geese, long legged or oven ready, available from end of September to December.

GREEN LABEL POULTRY
Loomswood Farm, Debach, Woodbridge, Suffolk IP13 6JW
Tel 0473 735456
Fax 0473 738887
Gressingham Duckling supplied as an ovenready bird, also Lunesdale Duckling. Both available whole, portioned, or smoked.

HEAL FARM QUALITY TRADITIONAL MEATS
Heal Farm, Kingsnympton, Umberleigh, Devon EX37 9TB
Tel 0769 574341
Fax 0769 572839
Additive-free non-intensively reared meats, including pork, venison, wild boar, smoked or green hams. Also supplies sausages, pâtés, bacon, and smoked products. Hamper service which includes non meat products such as cheese, smoked and fresh fish etc. List of products on request.

R&J LODGE
4 Green Ends Rd, Meltham,
Huddersfield, West Yorkshire HD7 3NW
Tel 0484 850571
Handmade pies in varieties including
pork, turkey and ham, and game. Packs
of assorted farmhouse cheeses.

MACBETH'S
20 High St, Forres, Moray, Grampian
IV36 ODB Scotland
Tel 0309 72254
Fax 034389 265
Naturally reared beef and game. Black
pudding and salmon also available. Gift
packs and hamper service.

IAN MILLER'S ORGANIC MEAT
Jamesfield Farm, By Newburgh, Fife
KY14 6EW Scotland
Tel 0738 85498
Fax 0738 89741
Organic meat including beef, lamb,
sausages, burgers, plus free range pork,
bacon, chicken and wild Scottish
venison.

THE PURE MEAT CO LTD
Moreton Hampstead, Devon TQ13 8QP
Tel 0647 40321
Fax 0647 40402
Additive-free meat and poultry. Leaflet
on request.

REAL MEAT COMPANY LTD
East Hill Farm, Heytesbury, Warminster,
Wilts BA12 OHR
Tel 0985 40501
Fax 0985 40243
Beef, pork, lamb, sausages, free range
chickens, bacons, hams, reared without
growth promoters or pre-emptive
medications. Prepared and packed to
customers own requirements.

SANDRIDGE FARMHOUSE BACON
Sandridge Farm, Bromham,
Chippenham, Wiltshire SN15 2JL
Tel 0380 850304
Wiltshire bacon available green and
smoked. Also dry cured hams and
gammons cured in cider and beer. Pigs
are reared naturally without food
additives or artificial hormones and
growth promoters.

SOMERSET DUCKS
Greenway Farm, North Newton,
Bridgwater, Somerset TA7 ODS
Tel 0278 662656
Fresh whole ducks, portions, smoked
duck breast, sausages, pâtés and pies.
Also boned ducks with stuffings.

TORDEAN FARM
Dean Prior, Buckfastleigh, South Devon
TQ11 OLY
Tel 0364 43305
Natural meats and poultry produced
without additives, antibiotic feeding and
growth stimulants.

UNIQUE BUTCHERS
217 Holloway Road, London N7 8DL
Tel 071 609 7016
Organic fresh pork, beef, lamb and
chickens. Can also supply organic
vegetables, breads and jams and game in
season. Home-made sausages in several
varieties. Minimum order.

WEST COUNTRY STYLE
Ashbeare Cottage Farm, Elworthy,
Taunton, Somerset TA4 3PY
Tel 0984 56389
Pork products including joints, bacon,
hams, traditionally cured and smoked.
Additive free.

RICHARD WODALL
Lane End, Waberthwaite, Millom,
Cumbria LA19 5YJ
Tel 0229 717237
Processor of traditional Cumberland
hams and bacon, also Parma ham style
air dried ham and Cumbria Mature Royal
ham. No chemical additives,
preservatives or extra water. Variety of
cuts and sizes.

SMOKED AND CURED FOODS

ASHDOWN SMOKERS
Skellerah Farm, Corney, Millom,
Cumbria LA19 5TW
Tel 065 78 324
Fax 065 78 339
Traditional cured and smoked foods
including sheeps', goats', cows' milk

cheeses, smoked meat, fish, game and
poultry. Brochure on request. Gift
service available.

BROOKSIDE PRODUCTS LTD
Block 20, Solway Industrial Estate,
Maryport, Cumbria CA15 8QU
Tel 0900 815757
Fax 0900 814606
Smoked fish and meat. Gift service
available. Minimum order.

BROWN & FORREST
Thorney, Langport, Somerset TA10 ODR
Tel 0458 251520
Smoked fish, including eel. Gift service.
Brochure on request.

GEORGE CAMPBELL & SON
FISHMONGERS LTD
The Smokehouse, West Harbour Rd,
Granton, Edinburgh EH5 1RF Scotland
Tel 031 552 0376
Fax 031 551 1149
Smoked salmon, gift wrapped.

CLEY SMOKE HOUSE
Cley, Holt, Norfolk NR25 7QT
Tel 0263 740282
Naturally smoked and cured fish
products. No artificial colourings or
flavourings used.

COLFIN SMOKEHOUSE
Portpatrick, Wigtownshire DG9 9BN
Scotland
Tel 0766 82622
Smoked fish, chicken and cheeses, also
gift and hamper service.

CORNISH SMOKED FISH CO LTD
Charlestown, St Austell, Cornwall PL25
3NY
Tel 0726 72356
Smoked fish, including offcuts suitable
for mousses and pâté.

FJORDLING SMOKEHOUSES
Dunstable Farm, Pitton Rd, West
Winterslow, Salisbury, Wilts SP5 1SA
Tel 0980 862689
Traditional oak smoked meats and fish.
No colours or preservatives used.

GLENDEVON SMOKED SALMON
Crook of Devon, Kinross, KY13 7UL
Scotland
Tel 05774 297
Fax 05774 626
Shetland Island salmon smoked over
oak shavings. Gift wrapped on request.

INVERAWE SMOKEHOUSES
Inverawe House, Taynuilt, Argyll PA35
1HU Scotland
Tel 08662 446
Fax 08662 274
Range of oak smoked fish, including
cod's roe, trout caviar and pâtés.

LOSSIE SEAFOODS LTD
Coulardbank Rd, Lossiemouth,
Morayshire IV31 6NG Scotland
Tel 034381 3005
Fax 034381 4632
Smoked salmon, gravadlax, smoked
trout and mackerel, kippers.
Presentation packs available.

MACDONALD'S SMOKED PRODUCE
Glenuig, Lochailort, Inverness-shire
PH38 4NG Scotland
Tel 06877 266
Fax 06877 311
Wide range of smoked fish including
barracuda, tuna, parrot fish, oysters and
scallops. Also cheese, quail and quails'
eggs.

MILL SMOKE HOUSE
Thornhill, Stirling FK8 3QE Scotland
Tel 0786 85348
Smoked salmon, trout, kippers and
chicken.

MINOLA SMOKED PRODUCTS
Kencot Hill Farmhouse, Filkins,
Lechlade, Glos GL7 3QY
Tel 0367 860391
Fax 0367 860544
Home oak cured fish, poultry and game.
Also supplies smoked wild boar, spiced
lamb, pigeon breasts, beef, even smoked
butter. Hampers available. Only smoked
salmon and gravadlax supplied by mail
order in December.

OAK SMOKED PRODUCTS LTD
Unit B/10, Hortonwood 10, Telford,
Shropshire TF1 4ES
Tel 0952 670180
Fax 0952 670037
Smoked fish and meat including salmon,
trout, gravadlax.

THE OLD SMOKEHOUSE
Brougham Hall, Brougham, Penrith,
Cumbria CA10 2DE
Tel 0768 67772
Smoked foods, available in hampers or
gift packs. Also handmade truffles.

PINNEYS OF ORFORD
Market Sq, Orford, Woodbridge, Suffolk
IP12 2LH
Tel 0394 450277
Smoked foods including wild Irish
salmon.

RANNOCH SMOKERY
Kinloch Rannoch, Pitlochry, Perthshire
PH16 5QD Scotland
Tel 08822 344
Fax 08822 441
Cured and smoked venison from wild
red deer. Also venison pâté, smoked
pheasant and grouse available.

RITCHIES OF ROTHESAY
37 Watergate, Rothesay, Isle of Bute PA20
9AD Scotland
Tel 0700 505414/503012
Fax 0700 505127
Smoked Scottish wild salmon, kippers,
smoked haddock and trout fillets. Gift
packs available.

SCOTTISH REEL
The Chandlery, Unit 2, 50 Westminster
Bridge Rd, London SE1 7QY
Tel 071 721 7424
Fax 071 721 7436
Smoked salmon, hand sliced whole sides.

RR SPINK & SONS (ARBROATH) LTD
33/35 Seagate, Arbroath, Angus DD11 1BJ
Scotland
Tel 0241 72023
Fax 0241 75663
Arbroath Smokies and Finnan Haddock
producers. Also supplies smoked
salmon.

THE WEALD SMOKERY
Mount Farm, Flimwell, East Sussex TN5
7QL
Tel 058 087 601
Cold smoked salmon, trout, eel,
haddock, chicken and sausages; all
additive and colouring free.

CHEESE

CURWORTHY CHEESE
Stockbeare Farm, Jacobstowe,
Okehampton, Devon EX20 3PZ
Tel 0837 810587
Three varieties of full-fat, semi-hard
cheeses, Traditional, Belstone and
Devon Oke made from farm's own
Friesian cows' milk.

FORTMAYNE FARM DAIRY
Fortmayne Cottage, Newton-le-Willows,
Bedale, North Yorks DL8 1SL
Tel 0677 50660
Sheep's cheeses supplied in 450-575g
(1-1¼lb) rounds. Wensleydale available
in 450g-2.3kg (1-5lb) rounds.

HURSTONE FARMHOUSE CHEESE
Hurstone Hotel, Waterrow, Taunton,
Somerset TA4 2AT
Tel 0984 23441
Handmade hard cheese, made with
vegetarian rennet. Cider from organic
apples in 2.2 or 4.4 litre (4 or 5 pint)
containers (or customers' own). Clotted
cream sometimes available.

ISLE OF MULL CHEESE
Sgriob-Ruadh Farm, Tobermory, Isle of
Mull PA75 6PY Scotland
Tel 0688 2235
Fax 0688 2140
Isle of Mull cheese, Cheddar-type hard
cheese made from unpasteurised whole
milk. Mini truckles of 225g (8oz) up to
full size cloth bound 24.3kg (54lb)
cheeses.

LLANGLOFFAN FARM
Llangloffan, Castle Morris, Haverfordwest
Dyfed SA62 5ET
Tel 03485 241
Cheeses made from organic milk and

with vegetarian rennet. Plain hard and red varieties.

LYNHER VALLEY DAIRY
Netherton Farm, Upton Cross, Liskeard, Cornwall PL14 5BD
Tel 0579 62244
Fax 0579 62666
Cornish cheeses in various sizes from 450g-3.2kg (1-7lb).

MILLWAY FOODS LTD
Colston Lane, Harby, Melton Mowbray, Leics LE14 4BE
Tel 0949 61371
Fax 0949 60030
Dairy-made Blue Stilton and Wyke Farmhouse Cheddar available by itself or in gift packs with a port or claret.

NEAL'S YARD DAIRY
9 Neal's Yard, London WC2H 9DP
Tel 071 379 7646
Fax 071 240 2442
Cheese specialists supplying produce from farms all over Britain. List on request.

SUSSEX HIGH WEALD DAIRY SHEEP PRODUCTS
Putlands Farm, Duddleswell, Uckfield, East Sussex TN22 3BJ
Tel 082 571 2647
Variety of sheeps' milk products including Feta, soft and hard cheeses, and cheeses flavoured with herbs, garlic or pepper. All products are made on the farm.

THE SWALEDALE CHEESE COMPANY
Mercury Rd, Gallowfields, Richmond, N Yorkshire DL10 4TQ
Tel 0748 824932
Additive-free handmade cheeses made from local Dales cows' and sheeps' milk. Smoked variety available.

HAMPERS

HL BARNETT
PO Box 200, Blofield, Norwich NR13 4AG
Tel 0603 715242
Fax 0603 713220

Gift service offering books, calendars, diaries, flowers, vouchers, hampers, foods, drink etc. All Christmas orders must be received by December 1.

BRIDFISH LTD
Unit 1, Sea Road North, Bridport, Dorset DT6 3BD
Tel 0308 56306
Gift packs and hampers of smoked products foods, wines, chocolates, and other gifts.

CALLY'S TOWN & COUNTRY COLLECTION
7 Hitchin Street, Baldock, Herts SG7 6AL
Tel 0462 892209
Fax 0426 892209
Hamper service offering unusual, handpicked gourmet products, including chocolates, wines, French herbs. Also offer special hampers for diabetics and other specialist diets. Gift service available. Brochure on request.

THE CHEESE AND WINE SHOP
11 South St, Wellington, Somerset TA21 8NR
Tel 0823 662899
Gourmet gift parcel service including wine. Gift vouchers also available.

CLASSIC HAMPERS
14 Upper Road, Higher Denham, Uxbridge, Middx UB9 5EJ
Tel 0895 832868
Fax 0895 835304
Selection of over 100 hampers. Brochure on request.

CLEARWATER PRODUCTS
Ludbridge Mill, East Hendred, Wantage, Oxon OX12 8LN
Tel 0235 833732
Fax 0235 835586
Gourmet food and drink products. Hamper and gift service available.

DAIRY HAMPERS
The Hamperage, Vansittart Rd, PO Box 66, Windsor, Berks SL4 5DZ
Tel 0753 851054
Fax 0753 831204
Hamper service. Brochure on request.

ALEXANDER DUNN & CO
Brook House, Bracknell Business Centre, Downmill Rd, Bracknell, Berks RG12 1QS
Tel 0344 411311
Fax 0344 860240
Gift service offering chocolates, wines, spirits, salmon, Stilton and other luxury items. Brochure on request.

EUROPEAN GIFT HAMPERS
32 Woodland Avenue, Hove, Sussex BN3 6BL
Tel 0273 555619
Fax 0273 509718
Tailor-made hampers in either gift cartons, wicker or picnic baskets.

FORTNUM & MASON PLC
181 Piccadilly, London W1A 1ER
Tel 071 734 8040
Fax 071 437 3278
Vast range of hampers. Send for brochures.

JAMES & JOHN GRAHAM LTD
Market Square, Penrith, Cumbria CA11 7BS
Tel 0768 62281
Fax 0768 67941
Speciality foods from Britain and Europe. Hamper service.

GRAYS OF WORCESTER
Valley Road, Merseyside L41 7FB
Tel 051 651 0251
Fax 051 652 0881
Food hampers, also range of gifts including Bonsai trees, flowers, champagne and gift vouchers.

HAMPERS OF BROADWAY
Cotswold Court, The Green, Broadway, Worcestershire WR12 7AA
Tel 0386 853040
Unusual foods, hamper and gift service.

HAY HAMPERS LTD
The Barn, Church St, Corby Glen, Grantham, Lincolnshire NG33 4NJ
Tel 0476 84420
Fax 0476 84777
Wines and gourmet foods in hampers or customised packaging.

HERITAGE HAMPERS
Hambleton House, 52 Church Lane,
Ormsby, Middlesborough TS7 9AU
Tel 0642 325050
Fax 0642 321566
Gourmet food and wine hamper service.

HIGHLAND FAYRE
Abernethy, Perth PH2 9JX Scotland
Tel 073 885 444
Fax 073 885 625
Gift and hamper service of Scottish food
and drink specialities.

HIGHLAND HARVEST
3 Cairnleith Croft, Ythanbank, Ellon,
Aberdeenshire AB41 0UB Scotland
Tel 03587 298
Scottish produce hampers containing
game, salmon, cheese and whisky. Can
be tailormade.

LEWIS & COOPER
92 High St, Northallerton, North
Yorkshire DL7 8PP
Tel 0609 772880
Gift packs, food hampers, glass and
chinaware in presentation packs.

THE OXFORD WINE & HAMPER
COMPANY
Hawthorn House, Rectory Lane,
Longworth, Oxfordshire OX13 5DZ
Tel 0865 820789
Fax 0865 821375
Hamper and gift service, also wines by
the case. Catalogue on request.

PRESENTS OF MIND
Berwick Barns, Terling Hall Lane,
Hatfield Peverel, Essex CM3 2EY
Tel 0245 381 220
Fax 0245 381 223
Gift service including champagne,
truffles, hams, smoked salmon plus
Christmas cakes and puddings.

QUADRANT HAMPERS LTD
Quadrant House, 91 Abbey Rd,
Dunscroft, Doncaster DN7 4LE
Tel 0302 350717
Fax 0302 350748
Christmas hamper specialists containing
a wide variety of fresh and packaged
food and drink products.

SELFRIDGES LTD
400 Oxford St, London W1A 1AB
Tel 071 629 1234
Extensive range of hampers, cakes, fruit
baskets and cheeses. Brochure on
request.

SHERWOOD LINK SERVICES
Link House, 141 Market St, Dalton in
Furness, Cumbria LA15 8RG
Tel 0229 62622
Fax 0229 63132
Champagne, smoked salmon, chocolates,
flowers and teddy bears, gift and hamper
service.

SPICERS
Unit 52, Lympne Industrial Estate,
Lympne, Hythe, Kent CT21 4LR
Tel 0303 262398
Fax 0303 261810
Fresh food hampers containing
traditionally cooked and prepared meats
and cheeses.

TRENCHERMAN HAMPERS
Hurst House, Hurst, Berks RG10 0SH
Tel 0734 342116
Fax 0734 320387
Fresh food hampers.

TURNER & PRICE LTD
Wiltshire Rd, Dairycoates Ind Estate, Hull
HU4 6PD
Tel 0482 54173
Fax 0482 565228
Specialise in Christmas hampers and can
send to overseas customers.

THE WINE SCHOPPEN LTD
1 Abbeydale Rd Sth,
Sheffield S7 2QL
Tel 0742 365684
Fax 0742 352171
Food and drink hampers in a wide price
range.

CONFECTIONERY

CHARBONNEL ET WALKER
11 Royal Arcade, 28 Old Bond St,
London, W1X 4BT
Tel 071 491 0939
Fax 071 495 6279
Chocolates, mints and other boxed
confectionery, also Christmas Puddings
and sauces. Brochure on request.

CLARKE'S OF LOCH EWE
Unit 2, Coldstream Workshops, Home
Place, Coldstream, Berwickshire TD12
4DT Scotland
Tel 0890 3153
Additive- and preservative-free handmade
chocolates. Gift service available.

GALLOWAY GOURMET FOODS
36a St Mary Street, Kircudbright DG6
4HZ Scotland
Tel 0557 31761
Fax 0557 31799
Handmade preserves, gift packed
confectionery, handmade chocolates,
hampers containing traditional Scottish
produce. Brochure on request.

GREAT GLEN FOODS LTD
PO Box 10, Old Ferry Rd, North
Ballachulish, Onich, Fort William,
Inverness-shire PH33 6RZ Scotland
Tel 08553 277
Fax 08553 277
Unusual Scottish food products
including Islay Tablet Scottish fudge and
ice cream made from goats' milk. Gift
service.

MELCHIOR CHOCOLATES
Chittlehampton, Nr Umberleigh, North
Devon EX37 9QL
Tel 0769 540643
Handmade truffles, pralines, liqueur
chocolates and chocolate animal shapes
as well as special Christmas lines. Gift
service available.

YE OLDE CHOCOLATE BOX
Prestbury, Cheshire SK10 4DG
Tel 0625 829645
Wide range of handmade chocolates
wrapped in presentation boxes and
packed in china items decorated with

ribbons and flowers. Hamper service.

TRUFFLES
Brougham Hall, Brougham, Penrith,
Cumbria CA10 2DE
Tel 0768 67772
Handmade truffles made with
Continental chocolate. Real cream, fruit
and alcohol fillings.

VILLAGE FAYRE
369 Uxbridge Road, Hatch End, Pinner,
Middx HA5 4JN
Tel 081 428 0202
Fax 081 421 2671
Handmade liqueur chocolates also
imported Belgian chocolates.

Cakes and baking

COOKIE CRAFT LTD
'Michaelmas' Common, Platt, Purton,
Wilts SN5 9LB
Tel 0793 770250
Home-made cakes including rich fruit
and sandwich and cakes made with beer,
mead and cider. Also cookies and
flapjacks. Gift baskets made up.

WILLIAM LUSTY LTD
Britannia House, Shaw St, Runcorn,
Cheshire WA7 5TZ
Tel 0928 569196
Fax 0928 580758
All kinds of cakes from Dundee and
Christmas to unusual combinations such
as rum and raisin, wild blueberry and
pecans, chocolate and mint. All cakes are
vacuum packed in tins and have a three-
year shelf life.

SARAH NELSON
Gingerbread Shop, Grasmere, Cumbria
LA22 9RH
Tel 05394 35428
Handbaked gingerbread.

THE OLD ORIGINAL BAKEWELL
PUDDING SHOP
The Square, Bakewell, Derbyshire DE4
1BZ
Tel 062981 2193
Bakewell puddings, handmade, supplied
fresh.

ORMEAU BAKERY LTD
307 Ormeau Rd, Belfast, BT7 3GN
Northern Ireland
Cakes, pastries, Christmas cakes and
puddings, Irish shortbread and savoury
baked goods, breads and oatcakes.

MEG RIVERS CAKES
Main St, Middle Tysoe, Warwickshire
CV35 0SE
Tel 0295 688101
Fax 0295 680799
Cakes, biscuits and brandy butter.
Catalogue on request. Hamper service
available.

SUGAR AND SPICE SCOTLAND
Whiteside Industrial Estate, Bathgate
EH48 2RX Scotland
Tel 0506 52493
Fax 0506 634714
Edible gifts and fine foods for all
occasions. Miniature cakes, iced cakes
with messages all available gift wrapped.

TREGROES WAFFLE BAKERY
Tregroes, Llandysul Dyfed SA44 4NA
Wales
Tel 0559 363468
Dutch waffles covered in Belgium
chocolate and filled with soft butter
toffee. No artificial additives. Wholemeal
and oatmeal variety with malt filling
suitable for vegans. Minimum order.

THE VILLAGE BAKERY
Melmerby, Penrith, Cumbria CA10 1HE
Tel 0768 881515
Fax 0768 881848
Specialist baker of organic bread,
confectionery, organic oatcakes and
flapjacks. Also Christmas puddings,
mince pies, rich fruit cake and
Cumberland Rum Nicky.

Jams and preserves

WENDY BRANDON
110 Stanford Avenue, Brighton BN1 6FE
Tel 0273 502947
Handmade chutneys, pickles and jams,
also flavoured oils. Products can be
made without sugar, without salt or
according to other customer

requirements. Gift service and brochure
available.

COTTAGE COOKING
The White House, Pebmarsh, Halstead,
Essex CO9 2NU
Tel 0787 269342
Fax 0787 224313
Mustard relishes. Varieties include
tomato and basil, coriander and lemon,
horseradish, and green peppercorn.
Table jars or miniature sizes in selection
packs available. Send large SAE for mail
order form.

HOBBS OF MAYFAIR PLC
PO Box 107, Bircham, Kings Lynn,
Norfolk P31 6RQ
Tel 0485 600619
Fax 0485 601156
Mostly Hobb's own label foods including
sauces, spices, conserves, jams, oils,
pickles, honey, nuts, tea, coffee and
confectionery. Supplied in hampers or
arranged on a ceramic plate.

LISLE'S HOME-MADE PRODUCTS
112 Cavendish St, Worcester WR9 3DX
Tel 0905 360303
Home-made lemon cheese made from
butter, free range eggs and lemons. Also
supplies jams, pickles and marmalades.
All products additive free.

THURSDAY COTTAGE LTD
Carswell Farm, Lime Kiln Lane, Uplyme,
Lyme Regis, Dorset DT7 3XQ
Tel 0297 445555
Fax 0297 445095
Raw sugar and whole fruit marmalades
and jams. Diabetic varieties made with
fructose available. Minimum order.

Miscellaneous foods

ABERGAVENNY FINE FOODS LTD
Pant-ys-Gawn, Mamhilad, Nr Pontypool,
Gwent NP4 8RG
Tel 0873 880844
Fax 0873 880250
Vegetarian and organic cheeses,
including goats', additive free meats.
Brochure on request.

ADNAMS
The Crown, High Street, Southwold,
Suffolk IP18 6DP
Tel 0502 724222
Fax 0502 724805
Importers and retailers of wines, spirits,
sherry, port, and champagne. Also oils,
vinegars, honey, mustard and other
condiments. Catalogue on request. Gift
packs available.

BERRYDALES SPECIAL NO CREAM ICES
5 Lawn Road, London NW3 2XS
Tel 071 722 2866
Fax 071 722 7685
Non-dairy, cholesterol and lactose free
iced desserts, suitable for those on
special diets or allergic to dairy
products. Supplied in 100 and 500ml
tubs. Min. order 5 tubs. Newsletter and
brochure on request.

BURBERRY'S FINE FOODS
18-22 Haymarket London SW1Y 4DQ
Tel 071 930 7803
Fax 071 839 2418
Confectionery, fudge, toffee, cakes,
puddings, teas, coffees, preserves,
biscuits, condiments. Brochure on
request. Hamper service.

CHURCH FARM SHOP
Strixton, Wellingborough, Northants
NNP 7PA
Tel 0933 664378
Organic, additive and preservative free
meats and meat products. Also sells
smoked fish, lamb and free range
chickens. Special packs of other organic
foods made up, such as dried fruits,
nuts, oils, tea and coffee can be made
up. Fresh fruit and vegetables service.
Brochure on request.

DENHAY FARMS LTD
Denhay, Broadoak, Bridport, Dorset DT6
5NP
Tel 0308 22770/22717
Fax 0308 24846
Farmhouse cheeses and cured hams.
Brochure, recipe suggestions, leaflets
available on request.

EXETER BEE SUPPLIES
Unit 1D, Betton Way, Moretonhampstead,
Devon TQ13 8NA
Tel 0647 40686
Fax 0647 40986
Honey sold in 450g (1lb), 225g (8oz)
and 40g (1½oz) jars, also packed in
Devon pottery.

FOSSE WAY HONEY
Northcote, Deppers Bridge, Nr
Leamington Spa, Warwickshire CV33 0SU
Tel 0926 612322
Honey from a variety of South
Warwickshire farms. Supplied in 1.4kg
(3lb) or 3.6kg (8lb) tubs.

THE FRESH FOOD CO
100 Bayswater Road, London W2 3HJ
Tel 071 402 5414
Fax 071 402 5414
Fresh free range poultry, conservation
grade meats, game, cheeses, coffees,
chocolates, oils, fish and shellfish. Boxed
or in hampers.

GRANT & MCLEAN LTD
Richmond Bridge, Galston, Ayrshire KA4
8JU Scotland
Tel 0563 820401
Fax 0563 821877
Smoked foods including trout and
salmon, cheese, venison, mussels, also
shortbread, whisky, fruitcake and tinned
Scottish specialities. Hamper service.

GREEN DRAGON ANIMAL FREE FOODS
Aber Road, Llanfairfechan, Gwynedd
LL33 0HR
Tel 0248 680267
Food products free from animal
ingredients eg soya, mayonnaise, soya
cheeses and spreads, egg free sauces.
Tailormade foods to order.

THE HIGHLAND CONNECTION
Earsdon Hill, Morpeth, Northumberland
NE61 3ES
Tel 0670 787392
Speciality Highland foods: fish, game,
preserves. Also Tartan rugs with water-
resistant reverse side. Hamper service
available.

JEROBOAMS
51 Elizabeth St, London SW1
Tel 071 823 5624
Cheeses, wines, charcuterie and oils
supplied individually or in hampers.
Other gift items available.

PAXTON & WHITFIELD
93 Jermyn St, London SW1Y 6JE
Tel 071 930 0250
Huge range of cheeses, also range of
hampers containing salmon, hams,
cakes, drinks, confectionery, pâtés and
other foods according to requirements.
Also own label sauces, jams and
chutneys available. Catalogue on
request.

ROSKILLYS CREAM & ICE CREAM
Tregellast Barton, St Keverne, Helston,
Cornwall TR12 6NX
Tel 0326 280497
Ice cream made from organic Channel
Island milk. 16 flavours, fruit ices and
non dairy alternatives available
throughout Cornwall. Fudges, preserves,
mustards and clotted cream only by
post.

THE SCOTTISH GOURMET
The Thistle Mill, Station Road, Biggar
ML12 6LP Scotland
Tel 0899 21001
Mail order club that supplies Scottish
produce and cooked dishes. Letter and
leaflet sent out to members each month.

SUMMER ISLES FOODS
The Smokehouse, Achiltibuie, Ullapool,
Ross-shire IV26 2YG Scotland
Tel 085 482 353
Fax 085 482 335
Wide range of smoked and fresh fish,
meat, game and poultry. List on request.

SUNRISE TRADING CO
29 Albermarle Road, York YO2 1EW
Tel 0904 653698
French foods including foie gras,
truffles, mushrooms, pâtés, terrines and
other specialities.

TASTEMASTERS & CO LTD
The Telegraph House, Lockerley,
Romsey, Hants SO51 OJE
Tel 0794 41082
Fax 0794 41082
British products made by cottage

industries. Range includes cheeses and English wines, sauces, hams, game and meats. Freezer packs and hampers can be made up on request. All goods are additive free and organically produced. Leaflets on request.

VIVIANS HONEY FARM
Hathersleigh, Okehampton, Devon EX20 3LJ
Tel 0837 810437
Wild flower and heather Devon honey supplied in glass or pottery jars. Cut comb honey also available at certain times of year.

WELLS STORES STREATLEY LTD
29 Stert St, Abingdon, Oxon OX14 3JF
Tel 0235 535978
Wines, cheeses and provisions. Selections and hampers can be made up on request.

DRINKS

CHAMPAGNE DE COURCY (UK) LTD
PO Box 50 Ashford Kent TN26 3YA
Tel 0233 861202
Fax 0233 610721
Champagne in half and single bottles, magnums and larger sizes, also cases of 6 or 12 bottles. Gift service available. Brochure on request.

VAL COLE (WINE BROKERS)
Unit 1, Marine Park, Gapton Hall Rd, Gt Yarmouth, Norfolk NR31 0NL
Tel 0493 667586
Fax 0493 657405
Mail-a-bottle service. Wine, champagne, or whisky with message and goblets or carnations to accompany.

DAVENPORT & SON LTD
The Courtyard, 52 Market St, Ashby-de-la-Zouch, Leics LE6 5AN
Tel 0530 412827
Fax 0530 412551
Wine, spirit or food gift packs and hampers.

DIRECT WINES (WINDSOR) LTD
New Acquitaine House, Paddock Rd, Reading, Berks RG4 0JY

Tel 0734 481711
Fax 0734 461493
Wines by the case. Personalised message and presentation packaging available. Minimum order 3 bottles. Brochure on request.

THE ORGANIC WINE CLUB
49 Fife Street, Dufftown, Banffshire AB55 4AP Scotland
Tel 0340 20995
Fax 0340 20995
Organically produced wines from all over the world. Minimum order.

YAPP BROTHERS WINE MERCHANTS
The Old Brewery, Mere, Wilts BA12 6DY
Tel 0747 860423
Fax 0747 860929
German and French wines, champagne also French oils and fish soup.

YEARLSTONE
Chilverton, Coldridge, Crediton, Devon EX17 6BH
Tel 0363 83302
Vineyard and cider apple orchard producing red and white wines and still, dry and medium sweet cider from undiluted juice. Individual bottles or by the case. Send SAE for list.

HERBS AND FLOWERS

BRADLEY GARDENS NURSERY
Bradley Gardens, Sled Lane, Wylam, Northumberland NE41 8JL
Tel 0661 852176
Herb nursery supplying 20 varieties of fresh cut herbs, suitable for freezing. Brochure on request. Min. order 50g.

THE HERBARY PRICKWILLOW
Ely, Cambs CB7 4SJ
Tel 0353 88456
Fax 0353 88451
Culinary herbs and edible fresh flowers. All produce organically grown and sold fresh. Special mixtures, eg bouquet garni, made to order.

POYNTZFIELD HERB NURSERY
Black Isle, By Dingwall, Rose and Cromarty IV7 8LX, Scotland
Tel 03818 352

350 varieties of culinary, medicinal and aromatic herbs grown organically. Supplied as plants, seeds or fresh bunches in season.

STEPHANSFIELD HERBS
Orrell Rd, Orrell, Wigan, Lancs WN5 8QZ
Tel 0695 632825
Suppliers of pot grown herbs.

SPECIALIST TURKEY SUPPLIERS

SOIL ASSOCIATION
86 Colston St, Bristol BS1 5BB
Tel 0272 290661
In early December the association produces a free list of approved suppliers of organically grown foods, including turkeys. Phone or write with an SAE. Available all year round are regional guides to suppliers of organic foods, although there is a moderate charge for these.

TRADITIONAL FARMFRESH TURKEY ASSOCIATION
5 Beacon Drive, Seaford, East Sussex BN25 2JX
Tel 0323 899802
Write or phone for a list of suppliers of turkeys bearing the association's Golden Triangle symbol. This denotes a bird that has been reared in open-sided barns, dry plucked and hung for 7-10 days to develop a richer flavour.

CAKE-MAKING EQUIPMENT

BR MATHEWS
12 Gypsy Hill, London SE19 1NN
Tel 081 670 0788

MARY FORD CAKE ARTISTRY CENTRE
28/30 Southbourne Grove, Bournemouth BH6 3RA
Tel 0202 417766

SQUIRES KITCHEN
Squires House, 3 Waverley Lane, Farnham, Surrey GU9 8BB
Tel 0252 711749

WOODNUTT'S
97 Church Rd, Hove, Sussex BN3 2BA
Tel 0273 205353/4

CHRISTMAS DECORATIONS AND MATERIALS

BRITISH CHRISTMAS TREE GROWERS
ASSOCIATION
12 Lauriston Road, London SW19 4TQ
Tel 081 946 2695
List of tree plantations around the
country. Send large SAE.

DAVENPORT MAGIC SHOP
7 Charing Cross Underground
Concourse, The Strand, London WC2N
4HZ
Tel 071 836 0408
Suppliers of snaps for crackers, as well
as other Christmas and novelty goods.

DECORPRINT LTD
4 Northwold Rd, London N16 7HR
Tel 081 241 1554
Decorations and stationery.

HOBBIES AND HANDICRAFTS
74 Coggleshall Road, Braintree, Essex
CM7 6BY
Tel 0376 550099
Kits for DIY decorations, candles,
mobiles.

PAPERCHASE
213 Tottenham Court Road, London W1P
9AF
and branches
Tel 071 580 8496
All kinds of decorative papers, cards and
decorations.

PAPER SAFARI
379 Upper Richmond Road, West
London SW14 7NX
Tel 081 876 5631
Papers and decorations.

THE QUILTERY AT McCALL'S
PO Box 27, Athey Street, Macclesfield
SK11 8EA
Tel 0625 429436
Steel stencils with Christmas designs for
making decorations, cards and table
settings.

QUINTO INTERNATIONAL
26 Warren Road, Guildford GU1 2HB
Tel 0428 714123
Old fashioned wooden tree tubs. Mail
order *only*.

THE SOUVENIR & DECORATIONS CO
Sondeco House, 1a Aldenham Road,
Watford, Herts WD1 4AD
Tel 0923 817227
Supplies bags, ribbons and sweet boxes.

Index

Page numbers in *italic* refer to the illustrations

almond whisky mincemeat, 78
apple and citrus mincemeat, 77
apple and orange mincemeat, 77
apricot and orange mincemeat, 78
cranberry mincemeat pies, 82
leftovers, 193
macaroon mince pies, 82
mince-pie parcels, 83
mincemeat and Cointreau flan, *149*, 150-1
mincemeat lattice flan, 83
mixed fruit and lime mincemeat, 78
pecan and almond mincemeat, 78
mini cottage loaves, 129
miniature houses, 42
miniature trees, 34, *35*
mixed fruit and lime mincemeat, 78
mixed lentil casserole, 188
mixed rice pilaff, *105*, 106
mixed spice sugar, 168
mixed spiced nuts, 124
mooli:
  mixed lentil casserole, 188
mozzarella, bacon and rosemary filling, 148
mulled wine, *65*, 157
mushrooms:
  ballontine of turkey, 106-7, *108*
  creamed leeks and mushrooms, *141*, 142
  lentil roulade with mushrooms, 111
  marinated mushrooms, 122
  mixed lentil casserole, 188
  mushroom and crab canapés, 125
  sprouts with bacon rolls and mushrooms, 103
mustard, home-made, 155

N

napkins, *36*, *36*, 37
nativity cribs, 51
neighbours, 116
New Year dinner party, 140-3
nutmeg sauce, sherry, 88
nuts:
  Christmas tree decorations, 16
  cinnamon sugared nuts, 178-9
  leftovers, 193
  mixed spiced nuts, 124
  pecan and Brazil nut topping, 75
  see also almonds; pecan nuts *etc.*

O

oils:
  herb and garlic, 165
  herb and saffron, 165
olives:
  marinated mushrooms, 122
  olives with pesto, 124
  roast goose stuffed with olives and prunes, *132*, 133
  vivid chicken with orange and olives, 184, *185*

oranges:
  apple and orange mincemeat, 77
  apricot and orange mincemeat, 78
  bitter orange chocolates, 178
  chocolate mille-feuille, 90-1
  Christmas tree decorations, 21
  fennel and orange soup, 140
  orange and chocolate logs, 174, *176-7*
  vivid chicken with orange and olives, 184, *185*
ovens, cleaning, 127

P

paint, Christmas tree decorations, 16
paper 'baubles', 18
paper hearts, 17, *17*
Parmesan and rosemary wafers, *128*, 129
parsley:
  lemon and parsley vinegar, 164
parsnips:
  sliced baked vegetables, 188
parties, 113-57
  Boxing Day buffet, 135-9
  checklist, 116
  Christmas tea, 147-51
  drinks, 123-6, 156-7
  gourmet banquet, 127-34
  hints, 116
  light supper party, 144-6
  New Year dinner party, 140-3
  party snacks, 118-22
  planning, 114
  quantity chart, 115
  spectacular centrepieces, 152-5
pasta, quantities, 115
pasta pillows, 191
peanuts:
  cheese and peanut shorties, 124
  mixed spiced nuts, 124
  pork satay, 123
pears:
  port-wine jelly, 92-3, *92-3*
  sticky upside-down pudding, 139
  Stilton and pear flans, 110-11
pecan nuts:
  pecan and almond mincemeat, 78
  pecan and Brazil nut topping, 75
  pecan and celery stuffing, 102
peppercorns:
  five-peppered beef, 154
  pepper vodka, 167
peppers:
  red pepper chutney, 160
  smoked salmon and peppercorn filling, 126
  spiced ratatouille salad, 109, *109*
  turbans of prawn and trout with pink peppercorn sauce, 130, *131*
pesto, olives with, 124
petal paste, 71
pickled satsumas and kumquats, 164-5
pickles, 159
pilaff, mixed rice, *105*, 106
pineapple:

cherry and pineapple glazed fruit topping, 75
  pineapple and date chutney, 162
pink peppercorns *see* peppercorns
pizzettas, 144-5
place cards, 116
plaice:
  rolled plaice with smoked salmon, 145
planning, 61-4, 114
plants, 34, 43
pomanders, dried-flower, 46, *46*
popcorn balls, 21
pork:
  ballontine of turkey, 106-7, *108*
  pork and herb bean pot, 182
  pork satay, 123
port:
  the Bishop, 156
  cranberry cocktail, 157
  raspberries in port, 165
port-wine jelly, 92-3, *92-3*
potatoes:
  chilled potato salad, 107, *109*
  crisp vegetable bake, 145
  curried potato and cauliflower casserole, 189
  diamond potatoes, *132*, 133
  fan-tailed roast potatoes, *101*, 103
  golden chicken and watercress bake, 192
  quantities, 115
  sliced potato bakes, 143
prawns:
  pasta pillows, 191
  salmon and prawn flan, 119
  salmon and prawn mille-feuille, *137*, 138
  turbans of prawn and trout with pink peppercorn sauce, 130, *131*
presents, wrapping *see* gift wrapping
preserves, 159
prunes:
  apricots and prunes in brandy, 166
  roast goose stuffed with olives and prunes, *132*, 133
puff pastry:
  pizzettas, 144-5
  raspberry Chantilly crowns, 134, *134*
  smoked ham and cheese mille-feuille, 136, *137*
punches, 156

Q

quantity chart, 115
quick Christmas tree rolls, 130
quick fruit cake, 76, *149*
quick lemon ice cream, 139

R

raffia tassels, 18
raspberries: